Prince William

Titles in the People in the News series include:

PEOPLE
IN THE NEWS

Prince William

by Terri Dougherty

Lucent Books, San Diego, CA

For my family

Library of Congress Cataloging-in-Publication Data

Dougherty, Terri.
  Prince William / by Terri Dougherty
    p. cm. — (People in the News)
  Includes bibliographical references and index.
  Summary: Profiles the eldest son of Great Britain's Prince Charles and Princess Diana, from birth to his acceptance at the University of St. Andrews.
  ISBN 1-56006-982-1 (alk. paper)
  1. William, Prince, grandson of Elizabeth II, Queen of Great Britain, 1982–Juvenile literature. 2. Princes–Great Britain–Biography–Juvenile literature. [1. William, Prince, grandson of Elizabeth II, Queen of Great Britain, 1982– 2. Princes.] I. Dougherty, Denis, 1963– II. Title. III. People in the News (San Diego, Calif.)

DA591.A45 W5554 2000
941.085'092—dc21

2001002791

Table of Contents

Foreword

FAME AND CELEBRITY are alluring. People are drawn to those who walk in fame's spotlight, whether they are known for great accomplishments or for notorious deeds. The lives of the famous pique public interest and attract attention, perhaps because their experiences seem in some ways so different from, yet in other ways so similar to, our own.

Newspapers, magazines, and television regularly capitalize on this fascination with celebrity by running profiles of famous people. For example, television programs such as *Entertainment Tonight* devote all of their programming to stories about entertainment and entertainers. Magazines such as *People* fill their pages with stories of the private lives of famous people. Even newspapers, newsmagazines, and television news frequently delve into the lives of well-known personalities. Despite the number of articles and programs, few provide more than a superficial glimpse at their subjects.

Lucent's People in the News series offers young readers a deeper look into the lives of today's newsmakers, the influences that have shaped them, and the impact they have had in their fields of endeavor and on other people's lives. The subjects of the series hail from many disciplines and walks of life. They include authors, musicians, athletes, political leaders, entertainers, entrepreneurs, and others who have made a mark on modern life and who, in many cases, will continue to do so for years to come.

These biographies are more than factual chronicles. Each book emphasizes the contributions, accomplishments, or deeds that have brought fame or notoriety to the individual and shows how that person has influenced modern life. Authors portray their subjects in a realistic, unsentimental light. For example, Bill Gates—the cofounder and chief executive officer of the software giant Microsoft—has been instrumental in making personal computers the most vital tool of the modern age. Few dispute his business savvy, his perseverance, or his technical expertise, yet critics say he is ruthless in his dealings with competitors and driven more by his desire to maintain Microsoft's dominance in the computer industry than by an interest in furthering technology.

In these books, young readers will encounter inspiring stories about real people who achieved success despite enormous obstacles. Oprah Winfrey—the most powerful, most watched, and wealthiest woman on television today—spent the first six years of her life in the care of her grandparents while her unwed mother sought work and a better life elsewhere. Her adolescence was colored by promiscuity, pregnancy at age fourteen, rape, and sexual abuse.

Each author documents and supports his or her work with an array of primary and secondary source quotations taken from diaries, letters, speeches, and interviews. All quotes are footnoted to show readers exactly how and where biographers derive their information and provide guidance for further research. The quotations enliven the text by giving readers eyewitness views of the life and accomplishments of each person covered in the People in the News series.

In addition, each book in the series includes photographs, annotated bibliographies, timelines, and comprehensive indexes. For both the casual reader and the student researcher, the People in the News series offers insight into the lives of today's newsmakers—people who shape the way we live, work, and play in the modern age.

Introduction

A New Standard for Royalty

WILLIAM OF WALES is a contemporary prince facing a daunting challenge. He has been raised to embrace modern ideals, yet is looked upon as the person who may be able to save a British institution that is twelve hundred years old. Constitutional monarchs are relatively powerless figureheads, symbolic leaders who no longer hold much decision-making authority. Now prime ministers are the leaders that implement change. This dual cost of government is being debated by citizens who view the monarchy as outdated. Though British taxpayers complain about the cost of supporting the monarchy, William is a fresh face for the royal family, an appealing star who has captured the public's interest. Many consider it his job to update the role of the constitutional monarch, making it less aloof and more appealing to the public.

William's parents, Prince Charles and Princess Diana, prepared William for this difficult task from the time he was a tot. They decided to give him a relatively normal childhood. Unlike most young princes, William interacted with children outside the palace and was treated by them as an equal rather than a superior. In contrast, Queen Elizabeth and Prince Charles had been raised in a way that set them apart from children their own age. Charles and Diana were determined to give William the opportunity to enjoy ordinary experiences, making him more in tune with his peers than his predecessors were. Whereas his father had led a sheltered childhood that left him disconnected from his own generation, William was able to mix with schoolmates and experience the simple joys of playing at a public playground, eating lunch at McDonald's, and seeing movies at a theater. As a result, he is able to relate to the people of Great Britain in a way his father and the queen are not.

Faced with the task of modernizing the monarchy, William already has experience in setting a new standard for royalty. He was the first royal to be educated in nursery school and primary school in a regular setting with other students, rather than tutored behind palace walls. He also chose his own college and coat of arms and decided he wanted to be called William rather than take the stuffy title of His Royal Highness while he was still in school.

Although William has had much more freedom than his father or grandmother enjoyed as youngsters, that does not mean he can ignore tradition. His family has allowed him to have a more modern upbringing than they had but still want him to take on the traditional role of king one day. There are duties and obligations that come with being a monarch, including attending official functions and greeting dignitaries. William had to learn to carry himself with

Prince William enjoyed a relatively normal childhood through experiences outside the confines of the royal palace.

dignity and to bend to the needs of the palace when necessary. As a youngster, even his play sessions were sometimes scripted, set up in a manner that allowed photographers to capture his playtime on film. William learned early on that his own feelings and desires had to be put aside at times in order to fulfill the role he inherited. As he matures, he will have to decide which royal obligations are worth preserving and which can be altered to fit his modern outlook.

The decision to allow William to flourish outside the palace has also meant that he has not been able to hide from the press behind its shelter. His mother was the most photographed woman on earth, and every outing with her meant camera lenses were pointed his way. William developed an intense distrust and dislike of the press at a young age, but since it can be an important public relations tool, he has learned to accept it as a necessary part of his life. The press has restrained itself from photographing his every move while he is a student, but as he matures he will have to be especially careful about how he handles himself. His actions are likely to be scrutinized, and will play a large role in swaying public opinion for or against the monarchy.

William is emerging as an independent, thoughtful, and kind young man with a good sense of humor and his mother's easy way with people. Self-confident rather than arrogant, he is at ease mixing with ordinary citizens at a local pub or with the upper crust of British society. He plays polo but is also a soccer fan, cheering for the Aston Villa team from Birmingham. The 6-foot-2-inch prince is not conceited about his dashing good looks and is uncomfortable with the rapt attention given to him by teenage girls.

Although William stands to inherit millions and has been called the world's most eligible bachelor, his appeal is greater than his money and social standing. William's engaging personality and level-headed, comfortable style make him even more endearing to the people of Great Britain and the world. Wealth and prestige will be his when he becomes king of England, but the flagging support for the British monarchy means he faces a weighty responsibility if he is to be certain of one day having a throne to inherit. William is not the first future king to have to fight for the crown, and he is ready to conquer his opponents with the weapons of diplomacy, grace, and charm.

Chapter 1

Contemporary Royalty

THE BIRTH OF Prince William was eagerly anticipated in Great Britain and around the world. His parents, Prince Charles and Princess Diana, had been married in a lavish ceremony on July 29, 1981, less than a year before his birth, and the wedding had revitalized the image of the staid royal family. The baby on the way represented hope that this rejuvenation would continue into another generation.

The British seemed rejuvenated by the anticipation of the birth of a member of the royal family.

Before the baby was born, it was clear that his or her life would be different than that of previous generations of royalty. When Princess Diana entered the royal family, she brought with her the ability to connect with the common people in a way that transcended her royal status and brought the monarchy closer to the people. Diana had been brought up in a wealthy aristocratic family, but before her marriage she had been a kindergarten teacher and had taken jobs cleaning people's homes and caring for their children. She was a beautiful, glamorous woman who placed a priority on helping others. She wanted her child to have an upbringing that was not stifled by the royal heritage that would make him or her aloof and disconnected from the people of Britain.

Charles had a traditional royal upbringing, which meant he was largely sheltered from the world outside the royal circle. He had a difficult time relating to others, had been miserable as a student, and did not want his child to have to endure the same painful youth. Charles and Diana were both determined to raise their child in a manner that included as many ordinary experiences as possible, even if it meant breaking with tradition to do so. William's parents were both familiar with how royal life worked and wanted to spare their child from the pitfalls of a sheltered upbringing.

Their Way

From the beginning of their family life, Charles, thirty-three, and Diana, twenty, showed that they wanted to do things their way. Queen Elizabeth wanted Diana to have the baby at Buckingham Palace, where her children had been born. Diana, however, insisted she have her baby in the hospital, where the latest medical technology would be available if needed. Diana's desire prevailed, and it was decided that the baby would be born at St. Mary's Hospital at Paddington in West London.

Charles and Diana took classes in natural childbirth, a birthing method that had become popular in the 1970s. Natural childbirth advocates the absence of pain-reducing medication during labor and involves the father in the delivery process. Previous generations of fathers had been relegated to another room while a midwife or doctor delivered the baby. During a natural childbirth, the father plays a crucial role in supporting the mother during labor.

A glamorous mother-to-be, Diana continued to remain in the public eye.

Charles was excited about the baby's birth and made it clear early on that he would be with Diana when she had the baby. "I am, after all, the father and I suppose I started this whole business. So I intend to be there when everything happens,"[1] Charles said.

Diana's labor was so difficult that an epidural injection was given to reduce the pain, but Charles stayed by her side through the last six hours of her sixteen-hour labor. Although it was no longer unusual for fathers to be in the delivery room during childbirth, for the prince of Wales it was a break from tradition in a family that was typically slow to change. Prince Charles's father, in contrast, had been playing squash with his private secretary when Charles was born.

It's a Boy!

On June 21, 1982, as word spread that Princess Diana was ready to give birth, the crowd outside St. Mary's Hospital steadily grew. The anticipation of the birth of the child who was destined to be

England's forty-second monarch aroused intense excitement and patriotism. William was already making a positive impact on popular support for the monarchy before he even took his first breath.

After 9 P.M., a cardboard sign appeared on the hospital gates with the words the crowd had been waiting for. "It's a Boy!" was written for all to see. Prince William arrived at 9:03 P.M., weighing 7 pounds, 1½ ounces. He was delivered by Dr. George Pinker, the royal surgeon-gynecologist.

The people outside the hospital chanted "Charlie, Charlie," asking for Prince Charles to come out and receive congratulations. They waved miniature British flags to show their enthusiasm. Two hours after William was born, Charles emerged from the hospital and shook hands with well-wishers. The crowd was exuberant, and the mood was one of adulation. Diana had brought new energy to the royal family, and the baby's birth continued to bring vitality as a new chapter in the lives of the monarchs continued to unfold.

Worldwide Celebration

The monarchy appeared anything but archaic after William's birth. Newspapers around the globe featured the news of the baby's birth on the front page. Bells rang and champagne corks popped in honor of the new prince.

The day following Prince William's birth was one of national celebration. The Royal Artillery produced a forty-one-gun salute, shooting off cannons in London's Hyde Park to honor the baby. The Royal Artillery also fired a salute in the nine-hundred-year-old Tower of London. Telegrams of congratulations arrived for the royal family from all over the world. World leaders as well as ordinary citizens sent flowers to them in honor of the occasion. The public's universal fascination with the royal family seemed to assure it a place in history for years to come.

At the Hospital

William didn't know anything at all about history as he rested comfortably with his mother in the hospital the night after his birth. The next morning he received his first visit from his royal grandmother, Queen Elizabeth. Wearing a lavender coat and hat, she smiled broadly at the crowd and the press as she entered the hospital.

Charles greeted her with a kiss on the cheek, and she spent twenty minutes visiting Diana and the baby. The queen's dress and decorum hinted at few of the changes that William was to bring to the royal family. She looked and acted her traditional regal part as she met the latest royal arrival who would one day reenergize the role of the symbolic leader of England.

When Charles met with the press later that day, he gave no hint about what the baby's name would be and explained that they were still not sure. Charles preferred Arthur, one of his names, or George, after his grandfather, King George VI. Not as bound to tradition, Diana liked trendier names, such as Oliver. The couple was in no hurry to decide, and it would be a week before the public learned the name of the new prince.

Royal Nursery

William left the hospital less than twenty-four hours after he was born to an approving crowd cheering, "Nice One, Charlie." With William wrapped in a white shawl, Charles and then Diana cradled

William's Name

Prince William's full name is William Arthur Philip Louis Windsor. It is traditional for members of royalty to have several names to honor other family members and their royal ancestors. William's first name comes from William the Conqueror, who was the first Norman king of England. The young prince honored his father with his second name, Arthur, which is one of Prince Charles's middle names. Arthur is also the name of the legendary king who was the leader of the Knights of the Round Table. The prince's third name, Philip, honored his grandfather, Prince Philip, the duke of Edinburgh, who is the husband of Queen Elizabeth. The name Louis came from close family friend (and Charles's great-uncle) Earl Louis Mountbatten of Burma.

William's last name is Windsor, a surname the family began using in 1917. Before then, the royal family had been known as the House of Saxe-Coburg and Gotha. The family thought the name sounded too German, however, and anti-German sentiment during World War I prompted the family to take the name of Windsor.

A strict genealogical interpretation of William's family name would have him go by the moniker Prince William Arthur Philip Louis Schlesweig-Holstein-Sonderburg-Glucksburg-Saxe-Coburg-Gotha. No wonder he prefers to be called simply William!

Charles and Diana were very loving, nurturing parents.

him in their arms and got into a waiting car. In contrast to his more
distant father, Charles was already a doting parent who could not
stop peering at his son's head as it poked out from beneath the
shawl.

Although William's parents wanted him to have normal childhood experiences, they did not compromise when it came to
William's material surroundings. Regal quarters awaited the baby at
Kensington Palace, the London palace where Diana and Charles
lived in a stately apartment. William slept in a hundred-year-old
cast-iron cradle in a nursery decorated in yellow and white. He
played with an ivory-handled rattle given to him by his great-
grandmother, Elizabeth, the Queen Mother.

Children's nurse Anne Wallace was available to help Charles
and Diana care for the baby, but Diana insisted from the beginning
that she play a major role in nurturing her son. She nursed William,
and by insisting on breastfeeding her child, she showed that she was
putting the baby ahead of her role as a princess. Bottle feeding would
have put his care more easily into the hands of others, and it would

have freed her from being at the beck and call of
breastfeeding gave her more control over his ca
tunities for the hugs and cuddles she wanted to g

Name Debate

In addition to the care of his loving parents, the new baby also needed a name. Charles and Diana's delay in naming their son only intensified the public's interest in the new baby. He had been called Baby Wales when he left the hospital, and guessing what name Charles and Diana would choose for their son became a popular pastime in Britain.

Bookmakers gave odds as people placed bets on their choices. George was the odds-on favorite, since George VI had been the father of Queen Elizabeth. The second favorite was James, also the name of former kings of England. The odds of the baby being named William were originally put at 5 to 1. However, by the time the name was announced, William came on strong and ended as the second favorite.

Finally, a week after the baby's birth, his name was announced. He would be called William Arthur Philip Louis. He was to be known as Prince William of Wales, and his first name could not be shortened in any way, a palace spokesman said, specifically noting that he would never be known as Billy. However, Charles and Diana softened these stuffy guidelines and nicknames evolved as the baby grew into a toddler. Diana called him Wills, while Charles referred to his rambunctious son as Willie the Wombat.

Baby Pictures

Although his parents were much more flexible than previous royal moms and dads, they could not always put their son first. There were times in William's life when duty was paramount. William would learn at an early age what it meant to put tradition above personal happiness.

He was christened on August 4, 1982, and during the photo session following his christening, he became hungry. As the session dragged on, he fussed and cried. Diana soothed him with her pinky so the photo session could continue, and Charles looked concerned and anxious as she attempted to comfort their son. William and his rents simply had to put up with the discomfort until the photographer was finished. There would be times when Charles and Diana put their son's needs above all else, but with the entire royal family assembled for a historic photo shoot, this was not one of them.

Doting Parents

On a daily basis, however, Diana and Charles made a determined effort to break with past royal child-rearing practices. They were constantly involved in William's upbringing, as opposed to past royal children who were raised more by nannies than by their parents. Queen Victoria, the mother of nine children, saw her small children for only an hour each day. Queen Elizabeth saw Charles briefly after breakfast, at lunchtime, and for half an hour before he went to bed. Although royal nanny Barbara Barnes arrived in August to care for William, Diana always made it clear that she and Charles would be making major decisions about his upbringing, and that she would always make time to cuddle her son.

Royal nanny Barbara Barnes holds the infant William.

Charles and Diana arranged their schedules around William. Diana spent every morning with the baby, and Charles often spent evenings playing with their young son and giving him a bath. As the baby got older, Diana began to take on more engagements but still made sure she had plenty of time set aside for her son. If she did not have an appointment, she would often spend the morning at home, working on her correspondence in a pink and blue sitting room with William nearby. When she had to be out for the day, Diana made sure she was back at Kensington Palace by 4 P.M. to have time to play with William before supper. Diana received many requests for appearances, but kept her schedule down to as few as three official visits per week so she could spend the majority of her time with William. She and Charles wanted to give their baby boy the security of knowing his parents would be there for him.

Trip to Australia

Diana's attachment to William was so strong that she could not bear to leave him for lengthy official visits to foreign countries. In the spring of 1983, the couple was scheduled to visit Australia for more than a month. Diana did not want to go that long without seeing her young son, even though it had been common practice for royal parents to go on lengthy trips without their young children. Queen Elizabeth had frequently traveled without Charles and his siblings, and the queen's own parents had left for a six-month trip to Australia and New Zealand when she was only nine months old.

Charles and Diana did not want to continue that pattern, but they did not know if they would be able to take William with them to Australia. A royal baby that young had never been on an official tour before. The situation was further complicated by the fact that those in line for the throne typically do not travel together, in case of an accident. However, Queen Elizabeth agreed that William could accompany his parents, and the prime minister of England encouraged the entire family to go. Nine-month-old William went on a six-week trip halfway around the world, becoming the first royal baby to go on an official foreign tour.

William and his parents may have been traveling together, but it was not a normal family vacation. William's nanny and his private bodyguard also accompanied the family. The airplane was equipped with a special suspended cot so the baby would not feel the airplane's movement and could sleep soundly. The family stayed in a regal ranch-style house in New South Wales, and the prince and princess were often busy making official appearances. However, every few days Princess Diana took a day off from her official duties to spend time with William. She knew she had to do her duty as a royal, but she also was committed to taking on the important role of mother.

Time Away

The trip to Australia and New Zealand was a success, but Charles and Diana were not always able to put their son ahead of their work. Sometimes their obligation to make appearances and visit foreign countries conflicted with the couple's ability to spend time with their son. Leaving William at home with his nanny was unavoidable at times.

Soon after their return from Australia, Charles and Diana were scheduled to take a two-week trip to Canada. The trip coincided with William's first birthday. Although it hurt them very much to be in a different part of the world as their son turned one, they decided they could not take him with them this time. The trip was relatively short, and the couple would be spending quite a bit of time on the royal yacht, the *Britannia*. They thought the rough seas and rocking of the boat would be difficult for William, and Diana had to be content with phoning twice a day to check how William was doing.

So, William spent his first birthday with his nanny, Barnes. A year earlier, his entry into the world had been celebrated with cannon fire and champagne. He spent the first anniversary of this event having a special tea with his nanny. He also did what babies normally do in the course of a day—he napped and practiced taking tentative steps while holding on to the side of his playpen. A more elaborate birthday celebration for the prince was held after his parents returned.

A Happy Beginning

William's first year had begun with celebration and jubilation as England and the world welcomed the young prince who began his

A successful trip to Australia was the first time a royal so young had traveled abroad.

life in the public eye. He was born into a family in which duty and tradition are paramount, but his parents were determined that his happiness and upbringing would not suffer because of their obligations. "The very fact that he sees so much of his mother and father and that they refuse to be separated from him—unless it is really necessary—is different from what even Prince Charles experienced,"[2] said Earl Spencer, Diana's father.

Charles and Diana showed their love to their young son by making him their first priority and by arranging their busy schedules to include as much time with him as possible. They sought to raise William as a contemporary royal, but could not get away from the fact that tradition played a huge role in their lives.

William grew from sleepy infant to gurgling baby to a standing toddler blissfully unaware of the effort it took to fill his young life with joy, happiness, and some semblance of what it was like to be an ordinary baby. Charles and Diana set aside royal customs to give William what he needed most at that time in his life: their love and attention. As William grew, they would continue to provide him with their affection and the luxury of learning what the world was like outside the confines of palace life.

Chapter 2

Untraditional Youngster

WILLIAM'S UPBRINGING WAS different from that of his royal predecessors. His public displays as a toddler were different from them, too. Previous royal offspring had stayed on the sidelines with their nannies and were only brought out to shine for their parents and the public when they were on their best behavior. Compliant, well-groomed behavior was expected at a young age. William's parents, however, did not want their time with their son to be so formal. They wanted to experience his every mood. They shared his laughter and playfulness as well as his tears and tantrums.

Because his parents' lives were so intertwined with his own, and because Charles and Diana wanted William to have more exposure to the world than previous royal children had experienced, the world had more exposure to William. When William toddled into the spotlight, his behavior was scrutinized. Newspaper reports about William did not always reflect positively on the royal family. As a typical toddler and preschooler, William tested his parents and nanny. He wanted to see how far he could push them before he was disciplined, and his independent, spirited personality provided some embarrassing moments for his parents. His temper and strong will led newspapers to dub him "His Royal Naughtiness."

William's antics included smashing a miniature picture of his ancestor Queen Victoria and nibbling an antique book. The young prince also had a fascination with flushing things down the toilet. He sent hankies and booties whirling out of sight, and even tried to flush a pair of his father's shoes down the loo.

Charles's and Diana's homes had security systems designed to protect the royal family from intruders, and William thought it was great fun to set off the security alarms that brought police officers to the palace. While playing in the Kensington Palace garden, he got away from his nanny and stepped through a beam of light that set off an alarm. At Balmoral Castle in Scotland, he decided to push an alarm button in the nursery.

Charles and Diana loved their son to the point of spoiling him, and they found it difficult to discipline their headstrong youngster. His nanny also indulged his strong-willed behavior. William once disappeared at the family's country estate, Highgrove. His parents and others searched, but no one could find him. He was finally located in the larder, a pantry where food is kept. William was drinking a huge bottle of cherry soda and had spilled most of it. Diana was relieved to find her son, but instead of punishing him for hiding and making a mess, she focused on the unhealthiness of the soda he was drinking. She did not like the artificial ingredients in the soda and banned carbonated drinks.

Although he was too young to realize the repercussions of his actions, William's naughtiness was putting a smudge on the royal

Prince William was a spirited and showy child, often attracting attention on public outings.

family's image. There is a thin line between cute and irritating where disobedience is concerned, and William had crossed over to the latter. The royal family feared that his behavior would affect the public's support of the monarchy, since no one wanted to put a "brat" on the throne. Even Charles admitted that William was a handful. At a nursery school, he told a teacher of three-year-olds, "I'll give you an hour with my child and you'll be worn out."[3] Although he and Diana hesitated to be strict disciplinarians themselves, they allowed William's nanny and bodyguards to correct his behavior.

William's independence had a positive side, too. It made him less anxious when he had to be separated from his parents. On a trip to Aberdeen, Scotland, when he was two, William had to travel with his nanny, while the rest of the family went on a separate flight. He was no longer a baby and had to travel separately from his father in case of a fatal accident. William did not seem to mind being away from his parents. During the flight, William played peek-a-boo with photographers and waved to other children on the plane.

Life at the Palace

Charles and Diana wanted to raise William to be aware of the world around him, but they did not deny him the privileges that went along with growing up in a wealthy family. William and his brother, Harry, were raised in a palace, and their parents' relaxed attitude toward their upbringing meant that they could take advantage of their spacious surroundings to have some fun. They enjoyed running in the long hallways and playing hide-and-seek amid the trees and flowers in the palace gardens.

Harry and William's bedroom was part of a two-room nursery in the attic of Kensington Palace. They had one room for sleeping in and another for playing in during the day. The boys also had their own bathroom, with a sink and toilet at their height.

Their nursery reflected both the ordinary and unusual aspects of their lives. It was filled with toys, but some were gifts from the leaders of foreign countries. Their nursery had windows to let in the sunlight, but the windows had bars on them for safety. The boys waved to their parents as they left for work, but instead of getting into a car, their parents sometimes waved from a helicopter on the royal helicopter pad outside the nursery window. William's family led a privileged lifestyle and lived in luxury. The tricky part for William's parents was to make him appreciate his comfortable surroundings and teach him to respect others who were not as fortunate.

With the arrival of Harry, William became an affectionate and protective older brother.

He snacked on biscuits and orange juice and enjoyed looking out the window. William was showing his well-behaved, adorable side, but he still had a long way to go if he was to give the British public a reason to keep the monarchy.

A Brother for William

The spotlight was taken off William for a brief time with the arrival of his brother. Henry Charles Albert David was born on September 15, 1984. His family called him Harry. The press showed a bit of flippancy by referring to the brothers as the heir and the spare. William was the heir to the throne after his father, and the arrival of his brother assured that the crown would stay in the immediate family if something happened to William.

William's behavior improved somewhat after Harry's birth, as did his public image. He was portrayed as the doting older brother who sat calmly during the first royal photo shoot for Harry and hugged and kissed his brother. His personality still had to be reined in at times, however. When the family took Harry to meet the royal butler and cooks, William hugged and kissed his brother so passionately that his nanny had to hold him back for fear that William would accidentally harm the baby. It was difficult for William to share the attention he was used to receiving with his younger brother, and he needed to learn to temper his enthusiasm and properly display his affection.

The "Basher"

William's bossy ways followed him to preschool. He was nicknamed the "Basher" because he pushed his way to the front of the line and was rough on the playground. When he did not get his way, he whined. He told a classmate, "If you don't marry me, I'll put you in my jail."[4] He also went through a phase in which he just could not keep from pinching women on the behind.

His public behavior was no better. When Diana tried to take him to his father's polo match near Windsor Castle without a nanny, it was a disaster. Diana tried to chat with Sarah Ferguson, who would later marry Charles's brother, Prince Andrew, but William incessantly pestered her. He kept asking Diana questions about where the horses and polo balls were. He demanded ice cream and a drink. He made faces if she did not do what he requested. He would not sit still, and she had to pull him back into the royal box by the seat of his blue pants. Twenty minutes into the match, she carried him to the car and they went back to the castle.

A Trying Time

Prince William's preschool years were a struggle for the youngster and his parents as he pushed them as far as he could to see what he could get away with. Though they meant well, his parents' affection led to an overly permissive discipline style that turned William into a spoiled troublemaker. A future king needed to be assertive, but he also needed to be properly behaved, even at a young age.

William's impish behavior came to a head at the wedding of his uncle Prince Andrew to Sarah Ferguson in July 1986. Despite fears that he would be unruly, four-year-old William was chosen to be part of the wedding party. On this formal occasion, it was William's job to follow the bridesmaids into the church, sit quietly through the

Weekend Getaways

William and Harry did not spend all their time at Kensington Palace. The royal family had several homes. On weekends, they often stayed at Highgrove, the family's country house in Gloucestershire, west of London. The boys had their own horses at the estate. William's was named Trigger and Harry's was named Smokey. When he tired of horseback riding, William could ride around in a miniature Jaguar, a gift from the car's maker.

On holidays, the family often visited the queen at one of her residences. Sometimes they saw her at Balmoral Castle in Scotland or visited her at Windsor Castle, west of London. Christmas was spent with her at Sandringham House, northeast of London.

service, and march out. He found it difficult to follow these orders. Dressed in a white sailor suit with a blue tie and a white hat, William fidgeted and squirmed throughout the ceremony. He also stuck out his tongue at the flower girls. His behavior had reached a point where something had to be done.

His Royal Cryness

A new, stricter style of discipline was needed for William, and to set the tone, a new nanny was hired. Ruth Wallace was brought in to help William control his temper and curb his strong will. Wallace was stricter than William's former nanny and would not tolerate tantrums in public. It did not take long for her to show William who was in charge. She reprimanded him at one of his father's polo matches because he would not stay where he was supposed to, and he was so upset that he burst into tears. A tabloid ran a picture with the headline "His Cryness."

For a while, William continued to rebel. When he was not allowed to blow out all the candles on the cake at a friend's birthday party, five-year-old William had a tantrum and threw sandwiches and ice cream around the room. He cleaned up the mess only when his nanny made him, and was taken home early.

William gradually learned to control his feisty spirit and transform his bossiness into an acceptable style of leadership. His mother was unswervingly supportive of the young prince. She was certain he would mature into a dignified young man who would be able to address the demands placed on him. "William is a proper

Searing Satire

William's naughty ways as a youngster were captured on the satirical British television show *Spitting Image*, a show in which puppets play the roles of members of the royal family and prominent politicians. One skit magnified William's unruly behavior, showing a William puppet, dressed in combat gear, attacking a Harry puppet with a knife and machine gun. Even though William was a preschooler at the time, the show's producers did not hold back as they portrayed him as a spoiled royal brat.

little gentleman," Diana assuredly proclaimed. "He opens doors for women and calls men 'Sir.'"[5] William's mother may have found it difficult to give William the discipline he needed, but she never had trouble giving him her love.

Another First

William's preschool years were notable for more than his difficult behavior. William set a new standard for royalty when he became the first member of the royal family to attend preschool outside the palace. Previous royal preschoolers had been tutored at home. Queen Elizabeth had been tutored at home for all of her schooling, and Prince Charles did not leave the palace for school until he was eight. Both had had limited contact with children their own age while they were young. In contrast, William's parents wanted him to mix with other children on neutral ground at a young age. They did not want to duplicate Charles's sheltered upbringing, which left him socially uncomfortable, shy, and insecure. Attending preschool with others would give William probably the only opportunity he would have to make friends who were unaware of his social status.

William attended Mrs. Mynors' Nursery School, near the family's home at Kensington Palace. In an effort to make him blend in as much as possible with his classmates, his parents asked that he be called William, instead of the more formal Prince William. His routine at school was the same as that of the other children in his class. He participated in counting, singing, and art activities in classes that met for three hours a day, twice a week.

There were still signs that his life was different from the other kids' lives, though. Because he was at the school, the building installed bulletproof windows, and detectives hung around during his classes. His classmates did not really understand what his prestigious background meant, however, and he was treated by them like any other child.

New School

After preschool, William's education continued at Wetherby, less than a mile from the family's home at Kensington Palace. He attended the private elementary school daily, dressed like everyone

William attended preschool with other children, consistent with his parents' desire to prevent him from being sheltered.

William is dressed in his formal school attire to attend Wetherby Elementary School.

else. He wore the standard uniform of black shorts, gray socks, a red tie, and a gray blazer and cap, both embroidered with the school crest. He studied reading, writing, and music, and was involved in competitive sports.

On a typical day, William had a schedule that mirrored that of his classmates. After breakfast, his parents kissed their son good-bye and he was driven to school in an unmarked car. School ended at 3:30 P.M., and he then had piano lessons, music-appreciation lessons, and private physical training instruction.

Charles and Diana worked to keep William levelheaded. Because his school had a uniform, he could not be a trendsetter who showed off his clothes to his classmates. He played with the same toys his friends did, and his mom sometimes drove him home in the family's Ford Granada.

The domineering personality William showed in his younger years gave way to a quiet confidence as he matured. He learned to balance his independence with the expectations of others. At a young age, he was showing the determination and self-confidence he would need to become a respectable representative of the monarchy.

Chapter 3

Maturing in a Broken Home

W ILLIAM'S STRONG, GROUNDED personality was an asset as his parents' marriage became more and more strained. Despite Charles and Diana's joint commitment to their sons, there were serious problems with their relationship. As their marriage faltered, Charles was linked with an old girlfriend, Camilla Parker Bowles, and Diana was rumored to have boyfriends. They tried to shield their children from the unpleasant mess they had made of their marriage, making it clear that they both loved their sons, but it was difficult to shelter their children from the pain they were causing each other. As both of his parents tried to look good to the public and have their sides of the story aired in the press, William could not be prevented from seeing how the two people he loved most were behaving bitterly toward each other.

His parents' emotional separation was clear when the family took a week-long trip to Canada in October 1991. The trip was an official visit in which Charles and Diana had many separate engagements. Charles was committed to promoting his causes, the environment, education, and architecture. Diana wowed the crowds with her beauty, grace, and kindness. When they were together, though, the couple rarely spoke. The boys kept a low profile on the 412-foot royal yacht, the *Britannia*, which was moored near Toronto. They were kept out of the public eye during the trip, which was a difficult one for the fractured family.

Separate Parents

As Charles and Diana grew further apart, the boys often saw their parents separately. Charles began taking on more duties and spent most of his free time at Highgrove. Diana preferred to live in London, enjoying the faster pace of city life while living at Kensington Palace.

Diana had more day-to-day contact with William and his brother, arranging her schedule around the boys' school calendar. Although Diana was busy and had distanced her life from Charles, she still managed to be a hands-on mom. She set limits on their television viewing, forbidding them to watch *Starsky and Hutch* because it was too violent. And even though Diana was afraid of horses, she took riding lessons so she could share that activity with her boys.

When Diana's duties took her away from her children, she called daily. She also made it a rule never to be away from them for more than three weeks at a time. When she returned, she greeted them with smiles and hugs and was not shy about public affection.

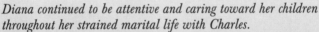

Diana continued to be attentive and caring toward her children throughout her strained marital life with Charles.

Diana and William enjoyed taking outings together. Here, they applaud during a Wimbledon tournament.

Unlike the more formal greetings royal parents had traditionally given their children in the past, Diana made it clear that this generation would not be treated stiffly and formally. Once when Queen Elizabeth returned from a three-month trip abroad, she greeted a young Prince Charles with a pat on the shoulder. Diana, by contrast, greeted her children with open arms. She had an unwavering affection for her children that gave them a sense of security.

As the boys grew older, Charles began to return to the more traditional role of a royal father who left his children's upbringing to others. He was more apt to arrange his life around his polo matches than his children's school schedules and enjoyed spending time in his walled garden at Highgrove, while his sons rode horses and played elsewhere on the grounds. He still loved and cared about his children, taking the time to see William's Christmas play and ride bikes with his sons at Highgrove, but he saw them less frequently as he paid more attention to the activities and duties required of him as a prince.

Attending Ludgrove

William got a measure of relief from his parents' difficulties in 1990 when he began attending boarding school at Ludgrove in Wokingham at age eight. He spent weekdays at the school, sharing a room with four other boys. His mom picked him up after school on Friday and he spent weekends at home.

William soon made friends at the 190-student school and became a popular student. He excelled in sports and became a leader among his classmates, honing the leadership skills he will need when he ascends the throne. He was captain of the rugby and hockey teams and also represented the school in cross-country running. He was a good shot and won the school's prize in clay pigeon shooting in 1994. He also acted in school plays and enjoyed reading.

At Ludgrove, William was sheltered from the media and was spared the full brunt of his parents' infidelities, which were being played out in the press. Television viewing was limited and newspapers were scarce at the school. However, the wily William sometimes sneaked into his bodyguard's room, which was adjacent to his own, to watch television or skim the newspaper before breakfast. Although the news was painful for him, he was curious about what was being said about his family.

Accident at School

William had one unfortunate accident at the school that led to worries about his health and highlighted his parents' marital difficulties. On Monday, June 3, 1991, another boy was swinging a putter on the school's putting green and accidentally whacked William on the forehead. William fell to the ground as blood seeped from a cut. A police car rushed him to the Royal Berkshire Hospital in Reading. When his parents were told of the accident, Diana sped toward the hospital in her green Jaguar from Kensington Palace, thirty-six miles away. Prince Charles, who was spending the week at the family's estate at Highgrove, was driven to the hospital in his Aston Martin.

His parents comforted him at the hospital, and William was brave and chatty as he was transferred by ambulance to London's Great Ormond Street Hospital later in the day. William had a depressed fracture of the skull and needed a seventy-minute operation to push out the dent. While he was in the operating room, the

William and Harry

William is very close to his younger brother, Harry. As with any brothers, there was a certain amount of competitive bickering when they were younger, but in general the brothers got along well. William has always looked out for his younger brother and has not hesitated to give him advice. Even as youngsters playing in a park one day, William advised Harry to take his jacket off so he could go faster on the slide.

Harry has an outgoing personality and a happy-go-lucky demeanor. Like William, he enjoys sports. Harry is a better-skilled skier than his older brother, and his superior talent once reduced a young William to tears on the slopes. Harry also enjoys playing soccer and cricket and riding horses.

William (left) and his brother Harry.

Harry often looks to William for guidance and support, which William has provided ever since Harry's first day of preschool, when William the veteran showed Harry the way to his classroom. William also showed protective concern for Harry after their mother's death and during his first press conference, when he expressed his hope that Harry would enjoy the same privacy he had while a student at Eton. William and Harry have a solid relationship, one that has become closer because of the difficult times they have endured and their unique positions in the world.

surgeons also checked for bone splinters and cuts on his brain. Serious complications such as epilepsy and infection leading to meningitis were possible. The surgery went well, however, and William suffered no ill effects from the accident.

William spent two days in the hospital, and his mother stayed with him the entire time. Ever the devoted mother, she felt her son needed her, so she canceled all obligations. She wanted to give him the comfort of knowing she was nearby.

His father, however, felt that it was his job to carry out his royal duties, no matter how worried he was about his son. Charles left the hospital while his son was in surgery, keeping an appointment to attend the opera. Later that night, he traveled north to Yorkshire for an environmental conference. He kept in touch by phone and visited William the following evening.

Charles was roundly criticized in the press for abandoning his son while he was injured. The headline in the *Sun* read, "What Kind of a Dad Are You?" Public support for Diana's attentive actions and disapproval of Charles's adherence to duty only pushed them further apart.

Distant Dad

Although the country could not understand why Charles would leave his son's bedside at such a trying hour, there is no evidence that William felt he was being slighted by his father. William accepted his dad for the man he was, a man to whom duty was paramount. Charles had become so used to putting aside his own concerns to attend to what he considered an all-consuming role, he

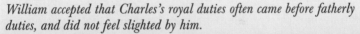

William accepted that Charles's royal duties often came before fatherly duties, and did not feel slighted by him.

did not think he was doing his son a disservice by leaving his care in the hands of the well-trained medical staff.

William was used to his father's absences. When he had returned home for a school vacation, one time, he had run into his father's study expecting to see him there. He burst into tears upon finding him gone. His mother called his father, who was at Balmoral Castle in Scotland, and Charles faxed a welcome-home letter to soothe his son. Charles still loved his sons, and enjoyed fishing and hunting with them, but he fell into the role of an aristocratic, upper-crust dad who leaves most of the child-rearing duties to the children's nanny.

Source of Strength

Charles also emotionally distanced himself from Diana, and William helped fill the void this left in his mother's heart. Just as his mother had stayed by his side while he was injured, William became her source of support as she dealt with the emotional effects of her crumbling marriage. When she was sad, he surprised her by calling San Lorenzo, her favorite restaurant, and reserving a table for her. He comforted her when she cried, pushing tissues under the bathroom door when she locked herself in and sobbed.

It seemed William was trying the best he could to find a way to solve the family's problems. He told a friend that he wanted to be a policeman so he could look after his mother. When a book was published that discussed Princess Diana's relationship with another man, William comforted his mother when she came downstairs from her room to see her sons. "William produced a box of chocolates and said, 'Mummy, I think you've been hurt. These are to make you smile again,'"[6] Diana said during a television interview. At a young age, William proved himself a compassionate son who had the inner strength to buoy his mother's spirits.

Separation

The public breakdown of his parents' marriage meant that William shouldered some very heavy personal challenges while a student at Ludgrove, and the boarding school gave him a circle of support as his parents' marriage failed. In November 1992, Diana visited William and Harry at Highgrove and told them that she and their father were separating after eleven years of marriage. Prince Charles spoke

Disney World

In 1993, the summer after Diana and Charles separated, Diana took the boys on a ten-day trip to Disney World. Their Disney vacation was not quite like the vacations other children enjoy there. For safety reasons, it was important for them to avoid the crowds. Their security guards did not want them to be in danger while they were having fun. To shield them from crowds, William and Harry were whisked to the rides in a motorcade through a series of secret tunnels at Disney World that are designed for VIP guests. And they got to go right to the head of the line once they reached each attraction. They were sliding down Splash Mountain only two hours after their plane landed in Orlando, Florida, and enjoyed Big Thunder Mountain and the Jungle Cruise before leaving for their rooms in the $1,450-a-night fifth floor presidential suite at the regal Grand Floridian. They were able to have a good time, even though security was tight. In order to blend in, some of their security guards were disguised as Disney characters.

to the boys about the separation when he visited them at their school. Ten-year-old William seemed quieter after his parents' separation. He kept most of his feelings about the matter to himself.

Although the failure of his parents' marriage was painful, it also added a degree of stability to William's life. It was clear that he would spend time with his mother at Kensington Palace and see his father at Highgrove. After the separation, Charles again became close to his sons. During the weekends and holidays they were home from school, they had scheduled visits with him. As William and Harry began to spend more time with their father, they learned to appreciate the quieter side of their privileged life. During visits with Charles at Highgrove and Balmoral, William and his father enjoyed hunting and shooting, and William liked watching his father's polo matches. They relaxed by fishing in Scotland. These visits with his father taught William to appreciate the more traditional side of his royal heritage.

When the boys visited their father, they were often with Tiggy Legge-Bourke, who cared for the boys and organized their days while they were with Charles. She enjoyed outdoor activities, and the boys hiked with her around the grounds of the family's country estates. Diana, however, was not fond of Legge-Bourke, and feared that she would become a substitute mother to her sons.

Learning Responsibility

Although she was separated from Charles, Diana was firm about continuing to play a large role in the upbringing of her sons. Even though William was an heir to the throne of England, Diana was not about to let the palace determine how he should be raised. She did not want to have her sons shielded behind a wall of stately decorum. She would continue to have a say in how they spent their time and whether or not they were ready to attend official functions.

Diana also made sure that William and Harry saw how the less privileged population lived. Volunteering in the community had been an important part of her education, and she made sure that her sons understood the importance of it as well. When Diana visited shelters for homeless people, William and Harry accompanied her when possible. The boys chatted and played cards with the people whose lives were so different from their own. These trips gave William a taste of what life was like outside regal social circles.

Diana and her son Harry get a splash from a water slide at Thorpe Amusement Park.

Diana continued to provide the boys with fun outings as well. They were allowed to dress casually, play video games next to kids their own age at Piccadilly Circus in London, and eat with their mom at trendy restaurants such as Planet Hollywood. They accompanied her to tennis matches at Wimbledon, and shrieked with delight at the thrill of going down a water slide at an amusement park. They also took a trip to Colorado, where they went whitewater rafting and rode four-wheelers.

Growing Up

William matured rapidly as he dealt with painful personal issues. He was strong and supportive, helping his mother through difficult times and growing closer to his once-distant father. The public end of his parents' marriage could not crush the strong spirit of a prince who remained steady as turmoil swirled around the House of Windsor. William showed at a young age that he could handle tumultuous change in his life, a trait that would serve him well in the years ahead.

Chapter 4

Life with the Press

WILLIAM WAS GROWING into a confident young man. There was, however, one aspect of his life that made him intensely uncomfortable. Every time William went out in public, the press was there, watching his every move. Reporters and photographers were almost constant companions of the contemporary royal family. As a modern prince, William was a sought-after subject.

The media is both a friend and foe of the royal family. Reporters and photographers provide the family with a way to show the public how active and involved they are in civic affairs, yet they are also bothersome because they maintain a constant presence and intrude into their family members' lives. Diana was especially favored by photographers, which meant that a cadre of cameras followed William on every outing with her. Leaving the security of the palace gave William knowledge of the world, but it also made him a target for the prying eyes of the press. He grew extremely wary of photographers and resented the way they chronicled his mother's every move. He had to learn to accept the fact that he would have to put up with a lack of privacy for the sake of the monarchy.

Early Press Coverage

William's experiences with the press began at an early age. Before he even knew what life in the spotlight meant, he was in it. The first official photos of William were made public a month after he was born, on Charles and Diana's first wedding anniversary. They were printed in newspapers and magazines around the world.

William starred in a press conference before he was a year old. Toward the end of his family's tour of Australia and New Zealand, pudgy ten-month-old William demonstrated his crawl on a rug spread beneath some trees at Auckland's Government House in New Zealand. His performance was a relief to Prince Charles's press officer, who had paced nervously before the demonstration, afraid that the clicking of the cameras would cause William to freeze.

At that time, the cherubic, twenty-four-pound William, dressed in a cream and apricot romper, was not bothered by the crowd at all. The energetic baby scampered toward a colorful toy. His proud parents were on either side of him, and Diana helped him stand and show off his thirty-inch height. He gurgled, and some reporters insisted it sounded like he said, "Da-da." William was unaware of the reason for the play session with his parents, and was so happy to have their attention that he did not mind a group of onlookers watching them.

Grooming Him for Press Coverage

Charles and Diana wanted William to be comfortable with the press. While they tried to allow him to be able to experience the ordinary joys of childhood, they also knew a royal child would generate an intense amount of interest from the media. Diana had

William's parents tried to make his early experiences with the press happy ones.

found it difficult to adjust to being constantly followed by a gaggle of photographers, and did not want her son to go through the same trying times. Charles saw it as his duty to provide the press with the photo opportunities to show the public what the royal family was up to. He and Diana wanted to prepare William for the fact that he would have to deal with the press throughout his life and wanted to help him learn to remain composed in front of photographers.

William did not worry about the press when he was young. As a toddler, he was taught to do the "Windsor wave," and on holidays he appeared on balconies and in carriages with his parents, waving stiffly to the crowds that assembled. By the time he was five, he was included in formal royal parades such as the Trooping of the Colour Ceremony, which marked Queen Elizabeth's official birthday.

Because of the public interest in his life, William's play sessions sometimes doubled as opportunities for photographers to get candid shots of the young prince. When he was five, he visited his grandmother at her Sandringham estate in Norfolk in January. William and Harry, along with their cousins Peter and Zara Phillips, got to climb around on a 1939 fire engine that had once belonged to King George VI, their great-grandfather. William wasted no time in putting on a fireman's helmet and ringing the bell. He was eager to play and did not care that his behavior was being closely monitored by reporters and photographers.

Dislike for the Press

William was oblivious to the press while he was young, but as he grew older he became more aware and resentful of its attention. Charles and Diana's hopes that William would be accepting of the press were only partly realized. William accepted the fact that he would need to be photographed, but it was a grudging acceptance. He disliked posing during photo sessions and was sometimes hesitant to participate. He reluctantly accommodated photographers as he posed with his brother and parents, but often needed to be reminded by his father that participating in the photo shoots were part of his duties as a prince.

The relentless press coverage his mother received wore on William. He hated the fact that he could not go out in public with her without being trailed by photographers. A walk from the car

William dons a fireman's helmet during a play session on an antique fire engine.

into a restaurant or theater set off the clicking of dozens of camera shutters. He dealt with it by ignoring the cameras, walking past them with his head down. William dutifully fulfilled his public appearances but still harbored a dislike for the press. He was cautious of being open with reporters and photographers and got upset when he saw the press or read about himself in the newspaper. He was aware of the problems the media had caused for his mother and disliked the press constantly bearing down on his family.

As Charles and Diana's relationship worsened, press coverage of the royal couple became more negative. More stories appeared about their infidelities, and both used the newspapers to make their sides of the story public. William saw the role the press played in the breakup of his parents' marriage and became even more distrustful of it. Diana and Charles knew how difficult it was for their sons to see stories about their crumbling marriage in the newspapers. Their 1992 separation was timed so that most of the press coverage would be over before the boys were home from school for

Christmas break. They hoped that William and Harry could be shielded from the brunt of the coverage, making the aftermath of their parents' breakup less painful for them.

Press Complaints Commission

Charles and Diana realized how difficult it was for their sons to have the press constantly chronicling the actions of the royal family and tried to give their sons' lives a degree of privacy. In 1995, British newspaper editors made an agreement with the Press Complaints Commission to not print intrusive stories or photos about Prince William and his brother while they were at school. In return, it was agreed that the palace would provide the press with some controlled access to information about the princes. Photos and interviews with William would be released at important stages of his life.

The privacy code had its roots in a ruling made when a newspaper in Accrington, England, interviewed a fifteen-year-old boy without the permission of his parents. The Press Complaints Commission ruled that this had been a breach of the editors' code, and decided that the privacy the schoolboy was entitled to also applied to the princes. "What goes for a child in Accrington goes for a child in Eton,"[7] said Lord John Wakeham, the chairman of the Press Complaints Commission. As a result, Prince William was allowed to complete his studies without having photographers following him everywhere. His private life, including his letters, e-mails, and telephone calls, were off limits to the media.

The agreement made William's life a bit easier as he prepared to continue his schooling at prestigious Eton, the British equivalent of a private high school. Thanks to the agreement with the press, he would be able to enjoy being a student and concentrate on his studies without worrying about having his every move monitored. Though he would still have to endure staged photo shoots and answer occasional questions about his life, he would be relieved of the pressure of being constantly followed at school. Having begrudgingly accepted the fact that he would have to share parts of his life with the public, William was thankful for the limits that were placed on the public's access to his private life.

Prince William's life appeared to be entering a period of stability as he reached high school age. His parents' shaky marriage had collapsed, but left in its wake a more stable family arrangement for William and his brother. He had survived a tumultuous time and emerged with a stronger sense of self, growing closer to his father while continuing to have a strong relationship with his mother.

Going to Eton

William again embraced the freedom of choice his parents offered him when he selected Eton College as his high school. Charles had wanted to go to Eton but had been sent to school at Gordonstoun in Scotland, where his father, Prince Philip, had also received his education. Whereas Philip had thrived in the stern setting, Charles had been miserable. He wanted William to have a more enjoyable high school experience and readily agreed to let him attend Eton, where Diana's brother and father had been educated.

Most of the students at the private, elite school are from upper-class, wealthy families. William was not the only student to have his

A Traditional School

In choosing Eton as his school, William selected a respected English institution. Wealthy families and dignitaries often favor the elite five-hundred-year-old school for the education of their children because of its solid reputation. The all-boys school of about thirteen hundred students is academically rigorous, and counts author George Orwell, James Bond–creator Ian Fleming, and poet Percy Bysshe Shelley among its alumni.

Eton has some traditions that can appear rather odd to outsiders. The dress code at Eton, which has been in place since the 1800s, is extremely formal. Younger students wear white shirts with stiff collars, black tailcoats, and pinstripe pants. Older students can wear special uniforms, such as bow ties, colorful vests, and houndstooth pants, if they are members of special groups such as Poppers, a group of popular students, or Sixth Form Select, the club for the most intelligent students.

The socks the students wear indicate how good they are at sports. Average students wear blue and black socks. Students who excel in sports are given a special color of socks depending on which student house they live in and which sport they are good at. There are 130 different colors of sports socks at Eton. Some students wear two different colored socks if they excel in two sports, as William did.

own bodyguard. Eton was a setting where William could blend in as best a prince could and be treated as an equal by his classmates.

Diana and Charles both accompanied William to Eton on his first day of school on September 6, 1995, and looked on with pride as William signed his name in the registry book. William's excitement and happiness with the school were evident as he proudly marched before photographers' cameras. Wearing the school uniform of dark tailcoat, vest, pinstripe pants, and stiff white collar, a smiling William looked confident as he walked with his classmates.

Time with the Queen

While Eton was a place where William could learn to mingle comfortably with his peers, it was also a place where he could be

William is dressed in traditional pinstripe pants and tailcoat to attend Eton College.

Rugby Injury

Part of the palace's agreement with the press allowed coverage of significant health issues involving Prince William. When he fractured his left index finger during a rugby match at Eton in early 1999, it was deemed a health issue important enough to merit press coverage. The injury, which was all the more irritating to the prince because he is left-handed, did not heal properly, and William needed an operation to repair it in April. Tiggy Legge-Bourke, along with the detective who always was near him for protection, drove him to the Derbyshire Royal Infirmary's Pulvertaft Hand Center for the operation, which was performed on a Saturday morning. The surgery went well, and William felt well enough to watch the Grand National horse race on television before leaving the hospital the same day. Although the injury was minor, it was of enough public interest that one newspaper's website included a diagram of the hand that showed exactly where William's bone had been chipped and described in detail how the bone fragment was held in place with pins, a screw, and wire.

William waves to the public after suffering a minor rugby injury.

schooled in royal tradition. Eton was conveniently close to Windsor Castle, one of the queen's residences. William only had to cross a footbridge from the Eton grounds to get to Windsor. He had tea with the queen most Sundays, and their discussions usually revolved around duties of "the firm," as the royal family referred to itself. During these teas with his grandmother, she taught him royal protocol. He learned how to handle himself in a dignified manner, how to treat others with respect, and how to act in public. William was encouraged to live as a modern member of the royal family, but at the same time was taught the importance of keeping the family's traditions alive.

William the Confirmed

William followed in the footsteps of his royal predecessors when he was confirmed at St. George's Chapel in Windsor in March 1997, becoming a full member of the Church of England. When he ascends the throne, he will lead the church as its supreme governor and take the title "Defender of the Faith." William had been given the liberty to make some changes with his royal lifestyle, but his family would not allow him to challenge tradition with respect to the church.

William's parents were coolly polite to each other when their fourteen-year-old son was confirmed. Their divorce had been made final the previous year, which gave a sense of closure to their strained relationship. Although Charles and Diana avoided speaking to each other, the atmosphere after the confirmation service was relaxed and happy. For the first time since 1993, Diana, Charles, and the queen posed for a picture together. Diana and Charles sat on either side of William for the official photo. The queen was comfortable enough to joke with the photographer and tell William's godparents they were standing too far back.

Charles and Diana arrived and left for the service in the same car with their sons. Charles drove, and Diana sat next to him. William seemed serious on the occasion, perhaps because he wanted to act properly and not cause a rift as long as things appeared to be going well. The family was ready to move forward with a new lifestyle.

Mother's Confidante

William continued to hold a special place in his mother's life, offering her comfort and advice. When the subject of her large wardrobe came up, he suggested that she auction off many of her dresses to raise money for charity. Diana gladly acted on his suggestion and in June 1997 auctioned seventy-nine of her dresses, raising almost $5 million to help patients at the Royal Marsden Trust Cancer Hospital. The clever, problem-solving William had found a way to help his mother and the community at the same time.

Diana was left tired and emotionally drained by the press's unrelenting coverage of her divorce, but she made it clear that she would remain close to her sons. As much as she would have liked to leave England and get away from the public scrutiny of her life, she knew she could not run away because of her commitment to her children. Diana commented that she stayed in England only because of her sons. "Any sane person would have left long ago," she said. "But I cannot. I have my sons."[8]

Mediterranean Cruise

Diana and her sons went on a Mediterranean cruise in July 1997 on a yacht owned by Egyptian billionaire Mohamed Al Fayed, the owner of Harrods department store in London and the Ritz Hotel in Paris. The cruise gave the boys a chance to relax and enjoy water skiing and sailing. The happiness the boys experienced with their mother on the cruise is tinged with sadness only in retrospect, in light of the impending tragedy that would shake the world as well as the royal family.

Also on the cruise was Al Fayed's son, Dodi, whom Diana began dating. Diana and Dodi spent more time together on the yacht in August, and finished their vacation with a night in Paris. Diana planned to be reunited with her boys in England the next day, but a car crash in a Paris tunnel never allowed her plans to be realized. The stability that had for a time graced William's life was shattered.

Chapter 5

William Conquers Loss

IN THE EARLY morning of August 31, 1997, Prince Charles entered William's room at Balmoral Castle in Scotland. Charles had been awake for most of the night after receiving the numbing news that Princess Diana had been involved in a car accident in Paris and had been killed. He broke the somber news to his son.

William, fifteen, went with his father to tell Harry. William dealt with his grief privately, remaining reserved and comforting his brother at that sorrowful time. The boys had been planning to meet their mother that afternoon. Now they would wait at Balmoral Castle with their grandparents while their father and Diana's two sisters went to Paris to retrieve Diana's body.

William and Harry spent the next few days mourning their mother's death in seclusion. They were in shock after the loss and needed time alone to come to terms with the tragic event that had taken their mother's life. It was especially disturbing to William that several photographers had been pursuing his mother's car at the time it crashed. She had seemingly paid for the press's insatiable appetite for her photo with her life.

The entire nation grieved along with the princes. Countless bouquets of flowers were placed outside the Kensington Palace gate in Diana's memory. The boys were devastated by their mother's death, but bravely appeared in public several days later to accept the condolences from the nation. Pale and subdued, they looked over the floral tributes outside the gate. Prince William graciously accepted bouquets and condolences from people in the crowd, grasping the nation's need to mourn the tragedy with him.

Diana's coffin rested in front of an altar in Chapel Royal at St. James's Palace in the days before her funeral and burial. William,

Harry, and Charles visited the chapel, and on Friday evening, the coffin was carried by hearse to her Kensington Palace home. A crowd of thousands lined the road as the boys and Charles followed the hearse in a limousine, looking somberly ahead.

Diana was buried the Saturday following her death. With bowed heads and grim faces, William and Harry walked behind the horse-drawn carriage that carried their mother's coffin. The coffin was covered with flowers, including a bouquet on top with a card reading simply "Mummy." The Royal Standard, the flag of the monarchy, was draped over the coffin. The princes were joined by their father for the last mile of the walk to Westminster Abbey, where the funeral service was held.

Diana's brother (left), sons William and Harry, and Charles attend the funeral for Diana.

Diana's brother, Charles Spencer, delivered the eulogy. He promised that Diana's blood family would try to protect William and Harry from having their lives immersed in duty and tradition. He did not want her sons to lose the freedoms she had insisted they be allowed to have.

The casket was then taken to the Spencer family estate, and Charles, William, Harry, and seven others attended the private family burial service on an island in the ornamental lake at Althorp Park. Diana was at rest. In her children, her legacy lived on.

Dealing with Grief

The British are traditionally unemotional people who keep a stiff upper lip in times of crisis. William was no different. In the months following Diana's death, William kept much of his grief inside. He returned to Eton after his mother's death, but did not let it appear as if anything bothered him. He did not speak about her and left the room when her name was mentioned on television.

While William was grieving the loss of his mother, others began to see his mother in him. William and Diana were both fair and tall, with good looks and a shy smile. Diana had a regal aura about her that William inherited. As the world missed Diana, people looked to William to carry on her memory. When he smiled shyly at an official appearance at Westminster Abbey on November 20, 1997, marking the golden wedding anniversary of Queen Elizabeth and Prince Philip, he provided a grieving nation with a glimmer of hope that the ambiance his mother had brought to the monarchy would continue in him. It also provided William with the difficult task of hanging on to his mother's memory while moving out of her shadow to forge his own identity.

Some went so far as to pin their hopes for the future of the monarchy on William. Whereas some questioned Charles's suitability to one day be king, there was no such question of William. Support for the monarchy had fallen after Charles and Diana's divorce; the actions of the prince and princess made the public question whether Britain had a need for a monarchy at all. William's growing popularity provided hope that the monarchy would withstand the torrent of bad publicity generated by his parents' actions.

Teenage admirers in British Columbia, Canada, greet William.

Pop Star Popularity

William was likely aware of the opposition facing the monarchy, and of the fact that he was becoming increasingly admired by the public. But he did not realize the extent of his popularity until he took a trip to Canada with his father and Harry in March 1998. The trip was supposed to provide William and Harry with relief from mourning their mother, but when he was greeted by a screaming crowd of teenage girls, the trip instead put additional stress on William. He awkwardly made his way through the throng of fans, enduring both the adoration of the girls and teasing from his brother.

He composed himself for a meeting with officials, however, and smiled as he tried on Canadian Olympic team outfits. He was even relaxed enough to clown around with a few hip-hop moves. Although he had been surprised by the crowds, he pulled himself together and was able to enjoy the moment.

Enduring Attention

Attention from the public was typically something William endured rather than enjoyed. He begrudgingly accepted it as a fact of royal life, knowing that in order for the media to leave him in peace at school, he would have to agree to be accessible at other times. However, in light of the media's role in the death of his mother, he became even more distrustful of the press.

On his sixteenth birthday, William agreed to let the public glimpse his personality by providing answers to written questions from a news agency. He revealed that he enjoyed art, like his father, and that he liked school and its formal uniform. It was difficult being in the spotlight, he said, and noted that he found it tough to deal with the attention shown to him by teenage girls.

William also said he liked rugby, soccer, swimming, water polo, and tennis and was already savvy enough not to name a particular movie or singing group as his favorite, saying only that he

William and Harry became closer to their father after their mother's death.

preferred watching action-adventure films and liked listening to pop and techno music. He did not want a musical group or movie producer to use his opinion for publicity. He was even cautious about naming what he liked to eat, saying that simple dishes and fast food were his favorites.

William's hesitancy to be forthcoming with the media did not dampen the press's enthusiastic coverage. One newspaper devoted a special Sunday section to him in honor of his birthday. In a show of determination to guard his privacy, William filed a complaint with the Press Complaints Commission to protest the coverage.

Closer to Dad

The press also ruined a surprise birthday party that William and Harry planned for their father later that summer. In the months after their mother's death, William and Harry had become closer to their father. They moved out of the apartment they had shared with Diana at Kensington Palace and moved with their father to York House, a suite of rooms at St. James's Palace. Prince Charles took on a more nurturing parental role following Diana's death, and the bond between him and his sons grew stronger.

William and Harry showed how close they had become to their father when they planned a surprise fiftieth birthday party for him in August 1998. With the help of Legge-Bourke and Oscar-winning actress Emma Thompson, they invited a hundred of Prince Charles's friends to see a comedy show they produced. Charles was honored and touched by his sons' thoughtfulness, even though the surprise was ruined when a newspaper published an article about the planned party. The event gave William and Harry the opportunity to publicly show their support and love for their father.

Godfather

William was likewise supported by his father and others in royal circles, as was shown when he was chosen to be godfather to Konstantine Alexios, the grandson of the former Greek King Constantine. In April 1999, the sixteen-year-old prince waved shyly to a crowd of teenage girls as he arrived and greeted King

Constantine. The former king is one of Prince Charles's old friends and is one of Prince William's godfathers. William, one of seven European royals who are godparents to the child, had his arm in a sling at the ceremony as the result of a sports accident. He appeared relaxed at the baptism, smiling and steadily holding the child with his healthy arm. William was taking on more royal responsibilities as he moved confidently toward adulthood.

"Prince of Wheels"

That summer, William sought both responsibility and freedom as he went through a teenage rite of passage—studying for his driver's license. He passed the written portion of his driver's exam the day after his seventeenth birthday and took driving lessons from a member of the metropolitan police driving school. The press was interested in getting pictures of William behind the wheel, so he obligingly got in and out of a Ford Focus a few times and showed off what he had learned by taking the car for a spin outside a house in Gloucestershire.

The day after the photo session, and five weeks after his seventeenth birthday, William took his driving test. He was accompanied by his bodyguard for the test in Cirencester, Gloucestershire, near the prince's Highgrove home. After passing the test, William was so excited that he jumped out of the borrowed Ford Focus and punched the air in delight. In a play on his father's title as Prince of Wales, newspapers dubbed William the "Prince of Wheels." Charles rewarded William by giving him a VW Golf to drive.

William proved to be a responsible driver and a kind motorist. When he and Harry saw a person with a stalled car in early August 1999, they pulled over and offered to help. William went to a nearby group of apartments to get a friend, and together they helped the man push the car to the side of the road. The car's owner could not believe he had been assisted by two princes, who treated the incident as no big deal. The man was so stunned that he could not even look the princes in the face because he did not want them to feel uncomfortable. William's willingness to help showed that he was not only down-to-earth but also responsible and caring enough to realize the importance of helping others.

Prince William gets out of a Ford Focus after taking driving lessons.

A Popper

William's personality also won him friends at school, where he was selected as a member of an exclusive group called the Eton Society. The group is also called the Poppers, because members first met above a lollipop shop, and is the most popular and envied group at the school. William's inclusion showed that he was well liked and admired by his peers.

Poppers are student leaders in the school who can fine other students and have the privilege of staying out later. The small group sets itself apart from other students by dressing in houndstooth trousers and multicolored vests, instead of Eton's regulation black vest and pinstripe pants. One of William's vests supported his favorite soccer team, Aston Villa, while some of his others had cat's eyes and large purple spots. To join the club, William had to participate in an initiation that involved "de-bagging," or letting other students tear off his pants, and being pelted with baked beans. William was not above doing silly things in order to fit in with his friends.

William at Eton

William loved his time at Eton, where he excelled in both academics and sports. He was able to blend in with the other students at the school, many of whom also came from wealthy and privileged backgrounds. Like other students, William lived in a dormitory, called a house, which had fifty students under the guidance of a housemaster. He stayed in a private room as other students did, although he also had a private bathroom.

William had academic classes in the morning and participated in sports after lunch. He studied chemistry, Latin, physics, art, music, and design. He also got to choose some of his general studies courses, and selected such diverse topics as cooking, motorcycle maintenance, and music technology.

William also enjoyed sports at the school and won the 50- and 100-meter freestyle swimming competitions at junior level. He was named captain of swimming and enjoyed the vigorous sport of water polo. William also played polo at Eton, a sport his father loved.

Like his father, William showed a talent for art. At the age of thirteen, his pencil sketch of a tall English house was chosen from among more than 250 student entries to be displayed in an exhibit at Eton College. *The Times of London*'s art critic said the artwork revealed sensitivity and confidence, and that William had a flair for drawing.

Eton also allowed William to experience the performing arts. His class went to see the Royal Shakespeare Company perform at Stratford-upon-Avon and he took part in school plays. When he had a small role in Shakespeare's *The Tempest,* a proud Queen Elizabeth and Prince Philip were in the audience watching their grandson and his classmates perform. Eton gave William the chance to grow academically and socially, as he stretched his talents and his mind.

Gaining Independence

William sometimes surrounded himself with a controversial crowd. He enjoyed going to clubs and sometimes hung out with an older group of friends, some of whom had been caught in possession of drugs. Although William was too sensible to try drugs, it tarnished his image in the eyes of the public and his family when he hung around with those who made the wrong decisions.

His independent nature got him in trouble with the queen when she spotted him at a Cartier polo lunch in the summer of 1999. William had neglected to tell the queen or his father that he would be there, which went against royal protocol. He was dressed like a modern teenager rather than a stuffy prince, sporting sleek black wraparound sunglasses that made him look chic but unregal. It was clear that he was a typical teen who wanted to be in control of his social life and attire.

Love Boat

William's emerging presence on the social scene was of obvious interest to the press. Since they were barred from covering his activities at school, reporters and photographers paid close attention to the royal family's vacations. They were especially interested when both William and Camilla Parker Bowles were included in the party.

Parker Bowles had been a close friend of Prince Charles since before his marriage to Diana, and some saw his relationship with her as the reason for the breakup of their marriage. William was formally introduced to her after his mother's death, and as she and Charles spent more time together, William appeared to accept her as a person who made his father happy. He considered her son, Tom Parker Bowles, who was several years older than William, a friend.

When Camilla Parker Bowles was invited to accompany the family on a cruise on the Aegean Sea in the summer of 1999, some saw the trip as an attempt by the royal family to gain public favor for her. There were reports that it was William's decision to invite her along. If she had his approval, it was thought that she might be more palatable to the public. William did not comment publicly on his relationship with Parker Bowles, but his close relationship with his father suggested that he approved of their being together.

The cruise was also of interest because of the friends William invited along. Teenage girls and boys were included in the party, which generated intense scrutiny from the press as reporters tried to determine whether any of the girls were William's girlfriend. Some journalists dubbed the cruise the "Love Boat," and christened the eligible women on board the "love boat lovelies" or "shapely shipmates." William and his friends remained silent on the issue, however, as he tried hard to keep his fledgling love life from being played out in the press.

Falling out of Favor

The press was also interested in Prince William's other nonschool activities, especially hunting. Royal hunting trips were often loudly

lambasted by animal rights activists, but William did not let that
stop him from continuing to practice the sport. Like his father, he
enjoyed hunting, and he shot his first stag in 1996 at Balmoral. He
also enjoyed shooting pheasant at the royal family's Sandringham
estate. William did not find it necessary to court public opinion and
was not about to bend his interests to suit the public's favor.

William was hurt, however, when some London tabloids ac-
cused him of dishonoring his mother's memory by hunting.
"Arrogance" proclaimed one headline after a hunting trip in late
1999, while another shouted, "Shamefaced." Diana had hunted
when she was young, but disliked riding and had lost her interest
in hunting. However, she had not disapproved when it became
clear that her sons enjoyed the sport.

William also received negative publicity when he and Harry
rappelled down a dam in Wales without wearing helmets. Their adventure with Legge-Bourke was caught on film by another visitor to
the area, and the pictures that appeared in the paper generated a
reprimand from the palace and safety experts. Climbing experts

William enjoys royal hunting trips with his father and brother.

said it was foolish for the princes to descend head-first down a 156-foot dam without wearing helmets. After the photos were published, the palace released a message saying that in the future the princes would take proper safety precautions when they participated in dangerous activities. William was a young man who enjoyed taking risks and making his own decisions, and he was finding out that those decisions did not always garner applause.

On the Edge of Adulthood

William grew into a confident young man following his mother's death. He had lost the guidance of the woman who had championed his nontraditional royal upbringing, yet was able to retain the freedom she had so earnestly sought for him. Somewhat sheltered from the press, William was able to concentrate on his schooling and mature without worrying about media exploitation.

Like many other teens on the verge of adulthood, William was balancing his family obligations with his desire to be on his own. He still spent vacations with his family, skiing at Klosters [Swiss ski resort] in winter and visiting Balmoral Castle in summer, but he also spent time with friends, sometimes including them in his family's activities. William grew closer to his father, who saw how a more relaxed lifestyle made his son much happier than he had been as a young prince.

William faced new responsibilities as he matured. A driver's license and car gave him freedom, but he also needed to balance his desire for fun with appropriate behavior. As he stood on the edge of adulthood, William needed to hold fast to the principles that would keep him on a steady course.

Chapter 6

Prince of Hearts

As Prince William's eighteenth birthday approached, there was speculation about his future. Some assumed that he would rebel against the confining conventions of the monarchy, as his mother had, while others suspected he would dutifully follow royal customs, in the style of his father. William's challenge was to do both, with his own sense of style. He needed to bring the best traits of his childhood into his adult life and independently establish his own place in the world. William had to be wary of both stifling traditions and comparisons to his mother in order to develop his own identity as a contemporary prince.

As William matured, he became more self-assured. He was more at ease in public, appearing confident and relaxed during a photo session at the Swiss ski resort Klosters, where he spent an April 2000 vacation with his father and brother. Charles, clearly proud of the boys, sat between his two sons, who put their arms around him, and smiled and laughed easily during the photo shoot in the Alps. William was more comfortable with the media than he had ever been, and even chatted with a television crew in a lunchroom while they were editing the footage.

Photographers from all over the world gathered to take pictures of the trio, but William was the most sought-after. He accepted this position with good humor. When a French photographer asked him to look his way, William replied, "Yeah, sure," and playfully turned the other way as British photographers chuckled. When he was asked how he liked the nightlife at Klosters, he coyly replied with a grin, "Wouldn't know, wouldn't know,"[9] a comment that one paper called his first public fib because of reports that the prince enjoyed karaoke and had been seen in a club at the resort. Although William was willing to let photographers be privy to a slice of his public life, he was still guarded when it came to his privacy and the fun times he enjoyed with his friends.

The People's Prince

More and more glimpses of William's fun-loving side were beginning to emerge in public. Earlier that month, William had surprised a crowd at a hotel in Durham, England, by singing the Village People's 1978 hit "YMCA" as part of a karaoke contest. William had been staying at the hotel with forty-one Eton students as part of a geography field trip. The visiting students challenged local residents to a singing competition, and the locals were impressed with William's courteous manners and humble attitude. He mingled with the crowd and complimented one local man who sang his rendition of Elvis tunes.

As William's eighteenth birthday approached, he was emerging as a popular young man with a good sense of humor. He avoided

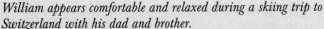

William appears comfortable and relaxed during a skiing trip to Switzerland with his dad and brother.

egotism and was so intent on fitting in with his peers that he declined to take the title His Royal Highness that could have been his when he turned eighteen. In a show of modesty, he asked to continue to be called by his first name. He also insisted that people did not have to bow or curtsey to him, feeling that this would put a barrier between him, his fellow students, and future friends. William planned to wait a few years before taking on a full slate of royal engagements and his title.

Eton Photos

William gave a gift to the media and the public in honor of his eighteenth birthday. To thank the press for leaving him alone while he was at Eton, St. James's Palace released a video and set of photos that offered a look at what the prince's life had been like while he was at the school. William agreed to the video and photos because he wanted to have some control over how his birthday was observed in the press. "I knew there would be a lot of media interest in my 18th and I didn't want a whole host of media involved," William explained. "Neither did I want any distractions as I was revising for my A-levels [exams]. So, I agreed to allow one photographer and a TV cameraman to spend a little time with me at Eton." [10]

The most popular photo showed William standing outside his house at Eton, wearing a traditional black tie and tails, the school uniform. His hands rested in pinstripe pockets. As evidence of his privileges as a Popper, he wore a colorful vest with a picture of the British flag and the *Austin Powers* catchphrase "Groovy Baby" instead of the plain vest that is part of the traditional Eton uniform. Some critics said he seemed to be bragging about his status as a member of the Eton Society, and argued that the Eton uniform only served to symbolize the rigidity of Britain's class structure. William was not intentionally showing off his aristocratic side, he was simply giving the public a glimpse of his life at school. As his world became increasingly intertwined with the lives of his well-bred, wealthy friends, he would have to make a conscious effort to remain acquainted with the less-privileged side of life that his mother had always insisted he experience.

Prince William proudly wears his vest depicting the British flag and the phrase "Groovy Baby" from the movie Austin Powers.

Trusted Photographer

William's decision to allow the public to glimpse his life at Eton showed that he was aware of the public's desire to know what his life was like. Once hesitant to work with photographers, he set aside his differences with the press and plunged into the project wholeheartedly. He realized that if he were to have some control over his public image, it was better for him to work with the press rather than fight it.

Photographer Ian Jones, who worked with the prince on the project, did not know what to expect from William when the project began. He knew that the prince had not been a fan of the press and was afraid he would be difficult to work with on this assignment. However, far from making the photographer's life miserable, William gladly accommodated him. They struck up a degree of camaraderie by discussing soccer teams.

The photographer found that the prince was upbeat and easygoing. They met in November of William's final year at the school to discuss the project; William was eager to share his ideas as well as listen to what Jones had to say. "His approach was mature and good-natured," Jones said. "I was very impressed."[11]

Jones spent three days with William over the next six months taking pictures of the prince in class, on the soccer field, and studying with friends. William became relaxed during the photo sessions, looking at the pictures on a computer as the project progressed. "He particularly liked the water polo shots, which I had done in black and white to capture the speed and drama of the sport," Jones said. "William liked how I caught how fast and furious the game is."[12]

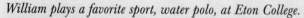

William plays a favorite sport, water polo, at Eton College.

Jones said the other boys at Eton treated William as one of the gang. "I found an intelligent, communicative 17-year-old who was fun to be with and work with," Jones said. "He seems very comfortable with himself." [13]

While William was open and friendly with Jones, he also knew when the prince had had enough. William cooperated as much as he could, but there was a limit to how much of his life he was willing to share. "There are times when he feels it is all too much and the shutters come down," [14] Jones said. William knew how closely he would allow examination of his personal life and had an inner drive to maintain control over it.

Granting an Interview

William also answered questions from Peter Archer, the Press Association's court correspondent, to mark his eighteenth birthday. William proved that he was adept at handling questions from the press without revealing anything too personal. As with the questions he answered on his sixteenth birthday, he was guarded about many details. He did not name a favorite author, singing group, or movie to avoid having his comments used by their publicists for promotional purposes. He also disliked being linked with show-business people such as Britney Spears. "There's been a lot of nonsense put about by PR companies," he said. "I don't like being exploited in this way but as I get older it's increasingly hard to prevent." [15]

William said media attention made him uncomfortable and was guarded when asked how he dealt with attention from girls. He said he coped with it "in my own way. Trying to explain how might be counter-productive!" Asked about a girlfriend, he said simply, "I like to keep my private life private." [16] William did say that he liked being with his friends, going to action films, and watching soccer and rugby games in his free time, but his answers were not long or detailed. He was allowing the public a glimpse of his life but made it clear that he wanted to guard his privacy at the same time.

Noting that he would stave off beginning royal duties on his own until he finished his education, William said he would at times continue to accompany his father on royal appearances. He was sketchy about his plans for the future, saying only that he would study art history at a university and that he had not really thought about whether he would enter the military after attending college, as his father had done. "At this stage I just want to get through university," he said. "I know there's been a lot of speculation but I really haven't made up my mind yet." [17]

William's comments about his future indicated that he would be the one making the final decisions regarding his role as a member of the royal family. Several times during the interview, he thanked the press for allowing him to make his most personal decisions in private, without the media and the public scrutinizing his every choice. "I've really enjoyed being able to go about Eton just as another student without the media attention," [18] he said.

William did not want his birthday celebration to be a big deal, and said he made no special plans. "I really haven't thought about it but no doubt I will celebrate privately with some friends," [19] he said. He ended up celebrating at a small bistro in Eton with forty friends. The guests grilled their own supper at the informal event in early June. William's commitment to being a typical student meant that he spent most of his actual birthday studying for exams. Although a joint party was given at Windsor Castle in honor of his birthday, the Queen Mother's one hundredth birthday, Princess Margaret's seventieth birthday, Princess Anne's fiftieth birthday, and Prince Andrew's fortieth birthday, William was unable to attend. The important college entrance exams he was studying for took precedence over the celebration. William decided that having a life like that of a peer was more important than royal functions.

First Press Conference

William could not always maintain an ordinary life. There were times when he had to use his role to publicly voice his opinion on issues he felt strongly about. And there was nothing more important to him than the memory of his mother.

William proved that he could handle himself with poise and self-assurance when he held his first press conference on September 29, 2000. Dressed like an ordinary teen in jeans, a sweater, and tennis shoes, he talked to the press in the garden at Highgrove with his father by his side. He bravely faced a contingent of reporters as he spoke out against a book about his mother written by Diana's former aide, Patrick Jephson. He said he and Harry "are quite upset

Though weary of the press, William continues to accept his place in the public eye.

that our mother's trust has been betrayed and that even now she is being exploited."[20]

The press conference marked the first time William had spoken in public about his mother. Before this he had been silent about the subject even among his friends at school. By defending her memory in public, William was taking another mature step and ending speculation about his feelings toward the books about his mother.

A second reason for the press conference was for William to discuss his plans for the year after his graduation from Eton. He planned to follow the English tradition of taking a year off from studies to travel and work abroad before attending university classes. His "gap year" would allow him to experience what life was like in other parts of the world and mix with people outside his social set.

Gap Year

William's gap year travels began earlier that summer in the Central American country of Belize. There, William joined the Welsh

Guards for nine days as they tackled a survival course. He switched gears from military tactics to marine conservation later in the summer when he spent three weeks on Rodriguez Island in the Indian Ocean to take part in an environmental study.

William's rigorous gap year continued in Chile, where he spent ten weeks in the fall of 2000 as part of a program sponsored by Raleigh International, a British group similar to the Peace Corps. Beginning in October, William and 102 other volunteers worked to haul lumber, teach English to local children, and do environmental preservation work. The trip was designed to give British students an opportunity to donate their time and energy in a part of the world that needed their help, but it also provided William with the chance to immerse himself in a project with teens whose backgrounds were very different from his privileged upbringing.

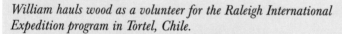

William hauls wood as a volunteer for the Raleigh International Expedition program in Tortel, Chile.

Volunteering in Chile

The trip began in a base camp in the mountains in remote northern Patagonia. The living conditions were vastly different from what William had experienced at home and at school. He slept on a makeshift bed in a classroom with fifteen others. They shared two toilets and a shower, and William had to help prepare meals for the group. "The conditions here aren't exactly what I'm used to," he told the British Press Association. "You share everything with everyone. I found it very difficult . . . because I am a very private person. But I learned to deal with it."[21]

William's willingness to adapt to the rugged conditions and blend in with the group earned him the respect of his fellow volunteers. His easygoing style helped him make friends in the group, and he was described as comfortable, genuine, open, and honest by a Raleigh International staff member. "He's got a very personable approach to life and has been happy to get stuck into everything and is very much a leading force within the group," said Malcolm Sutherland, the expedition leader. "His leadership has been excellent for someone his age."[22]

William resisted being set apart from his peers in any way and asked to be called Will or William. Many of the volunteers he traveled with were not from his exclusive social circle, so the trip gave him the opportunity to meet different types of people, including youngsters who were homeless or had been on drugs. Some were in an at-risk program and were not afraid to hold back their biased thoughts and feelings around the prince, including giving him the nickname "Little Princess." William took the nickname in stride and broke tension within the group by making jokes and cultivating peace between his traveling companions when it was needed. Most impressively, he insisted on being treated like anyone else. "I'm with a group of people I wouldn't normally be with and getting along with them is great fun and educational," he said. "There are some real characters in the group who don't hold back any words at all."[23]

The volunteers were there to help improve living conditions in remote communities and assist with environmental studies. William helped track the rare huemul deer as part of an environmental project and provided community assistance by carrying

William chops wood needed for the construction of a walkway in a Chilean village.

wooden supports and sinking them into the marsh to help the villagers build wooden walkways to link their homes. Another of his jobs was to teach English to schoolchildren in the Patagonian village of Tortel, a town about nine hundred miles from Santiago, the capital of Chile. He made the students laugh when he zipped his jacket and tucked his head down so he looked headless. The joke became even funnier when the zipper got stuck.

Struggling Success

Adventure was also part of the program, and it proved to be the most trying part of the experience. William and the group had to spend five rainy days on a lonely, foreboding beach. He slept in wet clothes in a small tent, as the wind howled, freezing rain fell, and everything he owned was drenched by the downpour. The group could not leave because the wind made the waves too big for their kayaks. As the wind blew so hard it threatened to blow the tent away, William and the others wondered why they had volunteered to go to such a place. "That was the lowest point," he said. " I don't think I've ever been as low as that."[24]

The weather eventually cleared, and William and the other volunteers had opportunities for fun. One evening, William acted as a DJ, broadcasting tunes from Bob Marley to Radiohead from a wooden hut. He also danced to a salsa band at a café and hiked in the Andes Mountains.

His favorite part of the trip was learning about the culture of the country he was visiting. The country's people, rather than adventure or learning about the environment, held the most interest for him. One of his favorite experiences was playing a makeshift game of soccer on the beach with a group of fishermen. Wearing boots and using fishing nets as the goals, the English group managed to win the first game. Unfortunately, William noted with a touch of humor, the locals won the next fifteen in a row.

William learned how fulfilling it can be to make a positive impact on the lives of others. Perhaps without realizing it, he was reinforcing the lessons of compassion his mother had worked to instill in him when he was young. He found that a genuine willingness to help could transcend language and cultural differences. "Here you are actually making a difference in other people's lives. At the same time, they invite us into their houses," he said. "It's the idea of getting along with someone even though there's a language barrier. Everyone here is so friendly, we all get on so well, and you don't need words."[25]

William's confidence grew during the expedition, and he emerged as a leader. The others lauded him for his tenacity and unpretentious nature. Although those against the monarchy dismissed William's charity work as a promotional tool designed to create a good relationship between the youthful, attractive prince and the public, those on the trip praised his genuine willingness to help. William was not afraid to venture beyond his social circle to widen his knowledge of the world and test his own limits as well.

Man of Action

William continued to push himself during his gap year. After spending a month working on a dairy farm in southwest England, he left for an adventurous three-and-a-half-month trip to Africa. As a junior game warden, he took on demanding physical labor such as mending fences, building shelters for park rangers, and fixing potholes. He also visited several countries to learn about animals and the environment. The trip solidified the prince's image as a well-traveled man of action who was not afraid to see what challenges the world had to offer.

Accepted at St. Andrews

Early in his gap year, William learned that he had done well on his precollege exams and had been accepted at the University of St. Andrews in Scotland. He had also considered going to college in Edinburgh and Bristol; with his choice he became the first member of the royal family to study at a Scottish university. Members

St. Andrews

When Prince William selected St. Andrews as the college he would attend, it had an immediate impact on the university. After he announced his intention to begin his studies at the school in the fall of 2001, the college was flooded with applications, particularly from young women who wanted to have a chance to get to know the handsome young prince. A good deal of these came from the United States.

It also became more difficult to obtain housing near campus. Several reporters rented apartments near the university before William began his studies there, hoping to establish a reporting base. This drove up real estate prices, making it more challenging for the school's students to find affordable places to live.

William is studying art history at St. Andrews, a school considered to have one of the best art history programs in Great Britain. The university, founded in 1411, is the oldest in Scotland. There are about forty-four hundred students in the university, which the coastal town of St. Andrews, a city of about sixteen thousand, is closely intertwined with. The university's buildings are spread throughout the city on the North Sea. Before Prince William announced his decision to study at St. Andrews, the town was best-known for golf, attracting players from all over the world to its dozen seaside golf courses. Thanks to Prince William, the town is getting more international recognition for its university as well.

In fall 2001, William began attending the University of St. Andrews in Scotland, where he is studying art history.

of the royal family had traditionally attended Cambridge; a committee had decided that Prince Charles would go to school there. However, in keeping with the desire of his parents to allow him to have some of the freedoms of a normal life, William had been able to make his own choice. He followed the lead of his housemaster at Eton, who was a St. Andrews graduate.

Academic achievement had not always been prized by the royal family. Queen Elizabeth did not go to college, and William did much better on his exams than his father had. Both studious and smart, William did not let his royal status allow him to become complacent, or use it as an excuse to avoid studying. His family supported him, excusing him from royal gatherings and duties when they interfered with his schoolwork.

William began his studies at St. Andrews in the fall of 2001, majoring in art history. That subject should not be a problem for William, who has works by Rembrandt, Vermeer, Canaletto, and Van Dyke hanging on the walls at his family's homes. William, who displayed talent as an artist while at Eton, fed his interest in art while at school, taking advantage of the abundance of masterpieces available for viewing in England's art galleries. William's school trips took him to the National Gallery, Royal Academy, Victoria and Albert, and Tate museums. He also learned about the business side of the art world when he spent time with an art dealership as part of a work experience course. Choosing an art history major allowed William to pursue a course of study that fit his interests and talents, and again to assert his independence.

Coat of Arms

William showed the world that he was proud of his regal background and that he still cared deeply for his mother, although he rarely saw his family, when his new coat of arms was unveiled. Coats of arms had originally been worn by knights, and are now used to symbolize a family or family member and authenticate documents. In honor of his coming of age at eighteen, William received his own coat of arms.

William's coat of arms shows a lion on one side and a unicorn on the other. These royal symbols both wear a small, red scallop shell on their necks in honor of Diana. The shell, which is also in the center of the shield and on the neck of the lion above the shield, is a symbol used on the Spencer coat of arms and was also used by Diana. It was an innovation to include a symbol from the mother's side of the family in the coat of arms, but William had input into the design and wanted to make sure his mother was remembered in his official symbol. His coat of arms was a mixture of his royal heritage and his mother's memory, and was symbolic of how William wanted to lead his life.

Most Eligible Bachelor

It was difficult for William to hold on to his mother's memory while establishing his own identity. He did not want to dismiss the good work she had done but knew it would extinguish his individuality if he was considered the new Diana. It was a particularly challenging task since the 6-foot-2, blond-haired, blue-eyed prince has inherited his mother's height, features, and charismatic style. "When I look at him it makes me shudder almost, because it's like looking at her," said press photographer Jayne Fincher. "He blushes in exactly the same place on his cheeks. The way he laughs. His eyes. It's uncanny."[26]

William's looks also meant that he had to come to terms with constant speculation about his personal life. The handsome prince has earned the title of the world's most eligible bachelor. Set to inherit a fortune and a glamorous job, he could lead the life of a playboy if he wanted. However, the levelheaded prince has developed too much self-respect to fall into that tempting yet immature role.

William has wisely been very discreet about his personal life. If he has a steady girlfriend, he has not been open about it. Although he was photographed "snogging" (British slang for kissing) a girl, he has been very careful to keep all details private, perhaps because he still remembers the painful sting of his parents' public relationship.

The Future

Tested and strengthened by difficult and tragic events, William is emerging as a contemporary royal who is preparing to lead the monarchy into modern times. Slated to follow his father as king, it

Handsome and levelheaded, Prince William is learning to balance the responsibilities of his royal heritage while maintaining some privacy.

will likely be decades before he ascends the throne. In the meantime, William needs to find a place for himself in the world in a way that signifies his love for his mother and the respect he has for his father and his royal heritage. But most of all, he will need to satisfy his desire to be an independent person.

The way William decides to lead his life will have a direct impact on the future of the monarchy, since his actions can easily sway public opinion to support or disapprove of the crown. If he behaves resonsibly, he will be able to carry out the royal duties for which he has been trained. If he takes his social status lightly and is irresponsible with the benefits of his privileged lifestyle, he will suffer for it. Prince William is a handsome young man on the way to being a superstar as well as king, and he must learn to deal with the responsibility that comes with those roles.

William does have some advantages that previous members of the royal family were not granted. Thanks to an upbringing that was relatively unsheltered for a prince, he will be more in touch with his generation than previous members of royalty. He also has the advantage of, for the most part, being able to direct his life as he sees fit and has learned to trust his instincts.

William's success as a monarch-in-waiting and as king will rest on his knowing what he wants and using his inner strength to fight for it. He has learned how to make his own decisions and has the self-confidence to continue to do so. His independence will be an asset as he establishes his own role in the royal family, a role that blends the lessons of unpretentiousness and compassion he learned from his mother with the royal traditions he inherited from his father.

Notes

Chapter 1: Contemporary Royalty

1. Quoted in Michael Demarest, "Rejoice! A Prince Is Born," *Time,* July 5, 1982, p. 1.
2. Quoted in Michelle Green, "A Royal First," *People Weekly,* June 27, 1983, p. 89.

Chapter 2: Untraditional Youngster

3. Quoted in *People Weekly,* "Harry and Di Are a Hit on Camera, but the Prince's Papa Is in the Palace Doghouse," October 29, 1984, p. 36.
4. Quoted in *People Weekly,* "The Guy's Smooth," October 3, 1988, p. 37.
5. Quoted in Leah Rozen, "His Brat Attacks Behind Him, Britain's Prince William Turns 5, Almost Old Enough for Long Pants," *People Weekly,* June 15, 1987, p. 124.

Chapter 3: Maturing in a Broken Home

6. Quoted in Robert Hardman and Richard Spencer, "I Had an Affair, Admits Princess," November 21, 1995. www.telegraph.co.uk.

Chapter 4: Life with the Press

7. Quoted in Matt Wells, "How a Boy Secured a Prince's Privacy," February 8, 2001. www.guardian.co.uk.
8. Quoted in Associated Press, "Princess Diana Killed in Car Crash," *Appleton Post-Crescent,* August 31, 1997, p. 1.

Chapter 6: Prince of Hearts

9. Quoted in Robert Hardman, "Prince William Puts on a Cup-Winning Display," April 8, 2000. www.telegraph.co.uk.

10. Quoted in Peter Archer, "Prince William in the Hot Seat," June 17, 2000. www.telegraph.co.uk.

11. Quoted in Elizabeth Grice, "Photographer Who Clicked with the Prince," June 17, 2000. www.telegraph.co.uk.

12. Quoted in Grice, "Photographer Who Clicked with the Prince."

13. Quoted in Grice, "Photographer Who Clicked with the Prince."

14. Quoted in Grice, "Photographer Who Clicked with the Prince."

15. Quoted in Archer, "Prince William in the Hot Seat."

16. Quoted in Archer, "Prince William in the Hot Seat."

17. Quoted in Archer, "Prince William in the Hot Seat."

18. Quoted in Archer, "Prince William in the Hot Seat."

19. Quoted in Archer, "Prince William in the Hot Seat."

20. Quoted in *Good Housekeeping*, "Prince William Between Two Worlds," July 2001, p. 96.

21. Quoted in *People Weekly*, "Chile Willy: Prince William, Rolling Up His Sleeves and Shedding Royal Prerogatives, Helps a Tiny Village in Patagonia," January 8, 2001, p. 72.

22. Quoted in Andrew Alderson, "Hard Work and High Adventure for William in Chile," December 10, 2000. www.telegraph.co.uk.

23. Quoted in Alderson, "Hard Work and High Adventure for William in Chile."

24. Quoted in Alderson, "Hard Work and High Adventure for William in Chile."

25. Quoted in Alderson, "Hard Work and High Adventure for William in Chile."

26. Quoted in Nancy Banks-Smith, "Tomorrow's Man," June 15, 2000. www.guardian.co.uk.

Important Dates in the Life of Prince William

1982

Prince William is born at St. Mary's Hospital in Paddington, London, on June 21.

1984

William's brother, Harry, is born on September 15.

1985–1987

William breaks with the tradition of home schooling for royals by beginning his education outside his home at Mrs. Mynor's Nursery School in West London.

1987

William enters Wetherby School, near his home at Kensington Palace in London.

1990

William attends boarding school at Ludgrove in Wokingham.

1992

William's parents, Prince Charles and Princess Diana, take the first step in dissolving their marriage by separating.

1995

William selects Eton as his high school.

1996

Prince Charles and Princess Diana divorce.

1997

Princess Diana is killed in a car crash in Paris.

2000

William graduates from Eton and holds his first press conference. He gives the public a glimpse into his time at Eton with video footage, photos, and a rare interview. He is accepted at the University of St. Andrews, Scotland, and spends his gap year going on international adventures and doing charitable work.

2001

William begins his studies at the University of St. Andrews.

For Further Reading

Books

Nicholas Davies, *William: The Inside Story of the Man Who Will Be King.* New York: St. Martin's Griffin, 1998. Large color photos highlight an engaging, detailed look at Prince William's life.

Michael Johnstone, *Prince William: The Story So Far.* New York: DK Publishing, 1999. Easy-to-read text and a cadre of large color photos make this book an enjoyable look at Prince William's life.

Randi Reisfeld, *Prince William: The Boy Who Will Be King.* New York: Pocket Books, 1997. A close look at William's life before his mother's death.

Periodicals

Michael Demarest, "Rejoice! A Prince Is Born," *Time,* July 5, 1982.

Michelle Green, "Ping-Pong Princes," *People Weekly,* September 6, 1993.

Kim Hubbard, Simon Perry, and Nina Biddle, "The Rising Son: Diana and Charles's Oldest Boy Emerges from Childhood with Her Stunning Looks, His Smarts, and All the Keys to a Kingdom He Will Someday Inherit," *People Weekly,* July 3, 2000.

Michelle Tauber, Simon Perry, and Nina Biddle, "Speaking His Mind: In an Unprecedented Press Conference, Prince William Blasts a New Diana Tell-All and Emerges as a Poised and Confident Future King," *People Weekly,* October 16, 2000.

Websites

www.guardian.co.uk. The Guardian Unlimited website contains a wealth of Prince William stories from England's *Guardian* and *Observer* newspapers.

www.royal.gov.uk/family/wales. An official site with information on members of the British monarchy, including Prince William.

www.sunday-times.co.uk. The online version of London's *Sunday Times* is another great source for up-to-the-minute information on Prince William.

www.telegraph.co.uk. The online version of England's *Daily Telegraph* has a wonderful archive of stories about Prince William and the latest information on the handsome young prince.

Works Consulted

Books

Mark Ellingham, ed., *England: The Rough Guide.* London: Rough Guides, 1994.

Robert I. C. Fisher, ed., *Fodor's Great Britain.* New York: Fodor's Travel, 1997.

Brian Hoey, *Monarchy: Behind the Scenes with the Royal Family.* New York: St. Martin's Press, 1987.

Anthony Holden, *Charles at Fifty.* New York: Random House, 1998.

Periodicals

Associated Press, "It's Prince William Arthur Philip Louis," *Appleton Post-Crescent,* June 28, 1982.

———, "New Baby Prince, Diana Doing 'Extremely Well,'" *Appleton Post-Crescent,* June 22, 1982.

———, "Princess Diana Killed in Car Crash," *Appleton Post-Crescent,* August 31, 1997.

Fred Bernstein, "William the Terrible: Di's Darling Is a Precocious Tot Who Can Be a Royal Pain," *People Weekly,* July 7, 1986.

Michael Demarest, "Rejoice! A Prince Is Born," *Time,* July 5, 1982.

Martha Duffy, "The New Royal Watch: Waiting for Wills," *Time,* December 21, 1992.

Good Housekeeping, "Prince William Between Two Worlds," July 2001.

Michelle Green, "A Royal First," *People Weekly,* June 27, 1983.

D'Arcy Jenish, "A Royal Canadian Sweep," *Maclean's,* November 11, 1991.

Bonnie Johnson, "Growing Up Royal: When It Comes to Raising England's Privileged Little Princes, Princess Diana Rules the Roost," *People Weekly*, April 25, 1988.

Louise Lague, "Questions for an Absent Father: As Diana Waited Anxiously at Prince William's Bedside, Faxmaster Charles Did the Usual—He Split," *People Weekly*, June 17, 1991.

Alexander MacLeod, "A Letter from London: Britain's Careful Crafting of a Future King," *Christian Science Monitor,* December 18, 2000.

People Weekly, "Chile Willy: Prince William, Rolling Up His Sleeves and Shedding Royal Prerogatives, Helps a Tiny Village in Patagonia," January 8, 2001.

———, "The Guy's Smooth," October 3, 1988.

———, "Harry and Di Are a Hit on Camera, but the Prince's Papa Is in the Palace Doghouse," October 29, 1984.

———, "Prince William: Britain's Dashing Young Royal Enters Adulthood and Makes Himself Heard," December 25, 2000.

Gwen Robyns, "Diana: When a Princess Becomes a Superstar! (Everything You Always Wanted to Know About Princess Diana)," *Ladies Home Journal,* June 1983.

Leah Rozen, "His Brat Attacks Behind Him, Britain's Prince William Turns 5, Almost Old Enough for Long Pants," *People Weekly,* June 15, 1987.

Internet Sources

Andrew Alderson, "Hard Work and High Adventure for William in Chile," December 10, 2000. www.telegraph.co.uk.

———, "Prince William 'Devastated' Over Diana Hunt Slur," December 5, 1999. www.telegraph.co.uk.

Peter Archer, "Prince William in the Hot Seat," June 17, 2000. www.telegraph.co.uk.

Nancy Banks-Smith, "Tomorrow's Man," June 15, 2000. www.guardian.co.uk.

Sandra Barwick, "He's the Height of Elegance, Just Like Diana," June 17, 2000. www.telegraph.co.uk.

———, "Our Colourful Prince of Pop," June 17, 2000. www.telegraph.co.uk.

———, "Panic as Princely Paella Survives Flood," June 17, 2000. www.telegraph.co.uk.

Stephen Bates, "A Private William Speaks Publicly for the First Time," June 17, 2000. www.guardian.co.uk.

———, "William Makes the Grade," August 18, 2000. www.guardian.co.uk.

Emma Brockes, "How Do You Like Me?" December 6, 2000. www.guardian.co.uk.

Derek Brown, "Prince William's 18th Birthday," June 21, 2000. www.guardian.co.uk.

Maurice Chittenden, "William Crowns Gap Year with Three-Month African Safari," March 4, 2001. www.sunday-times.co.uk.

Caroline Davies, "Sporting Prince William Shoots His First Stag," November 27, 1996. www.telegraph.co.uk.

David Graves, " 'Safety First' in Future for Daring Princes," August 10, 1998. www.telegraph.co.uk.

———, "William on Eton, Girls, and Life at 16," June 20, 1998. www.telegraph.co.uk.

Elizabeth Grice, "Photographer Who Clicked with the Prince," June 17, 2000. www.telegraph.co.uk.

Robert Hardman, "Just (Call Me) William," June 17, 2000. www.telegraph.co.uk.

———, "The Plaster Cast Prince Makes His Solo Debut at Royal Christening,"April 16, 1999. www.telegraph.co.uk.

———, "Princes' Birthday Respects to Diana," June 9, 1998. www.telegraph.co.uk.

———, "Princes Put on a Show for Father's 50th," August 1, 1998. www.telegraph.co.uk.

———, "Prince William Puts on a Cup-Winning Display," April 8, 2000. www.telegraph.co.uk.

———, "Surgeon Pleased with Operation on Prince's Finger," April 13, 1999. www.telegraph.co.uk.

————, "William Hits at 'Betrayal' by Author," September 30, 2000. www.telegraph.co.uk.

Robert Hardman and Paul Anast, "All Aboard for a Royal Cruise to Remember," August 6, 1999. www.telegraph.co.uk.

Robert Hardman and Richard Spencer, "I Had an Affair, Admits Princess," November 21, 1995. www.telegraph.co.uk.

Lee Elliot Major, "Prince William Effect Boosts Applications to St. Andrews," January 26, 2001. www.guardian.co.uk.

"Memory of Diana in William's Arms," July 10, 2000. www.telegraph.co.uk.

Stuart Miller, "Princes Rally Round to Help Driver Push His Stranded Car," August 5, 1999. www.guardian.co.uk.

Christopher Morgan, "William Dives into Gap Year on Coral Reef," September 3, 2000. www.sunday-times.co.uk.

Christopher Morgan and Humfrey Hunter, "William Plans 18th Birthday Sizzler," June 4, 2000. www.sunday-times.co.uk.

Christopher Morgan and Adam Nathan, "William, Prince of Karaoke, Is a Hit with the Village People," April 2, 2000. www.sunday-times.co.uk.

Christopher Morgan and Michael Prescott, "Charles and William in Nightclub Row," February 6, 2000. www.sunday-times.co.uk.

Alison Roberts, "You're Sexy Wills, But So Is a Republic," December 13, 2000. www.guardian.co.uk.

Andrew Roberts, "A Very Different Sort of Royal Upbringing," June 11, 2000. www.telegraph.co.uk.

Ben Summerskill, "Walks, Work, and Kayaking—Prince Mucks in on Chile Trip," December 10, 2000. www.guardian.co.uk.

Tom Utley, "Togetherness for Prince William's Confirmation," March 10, 1997. www.telegraph.co.uk.

Matt Wells, "How a Boy Secured a Prince's Privacy," February 8, 2001. www.guardian.co.uk.

Richard Woods, "William Hones His Royal Survival Skills," December 10, 2000. www.sunday-times.co.uk.

Index

Picture Credits

About the Author

Terri Dougherty is a freelance writer from Appleton, Wisconsin. In addition to nonfiction books for children, she also writes magazine and newspaper articles. A native of Black Creek, Wisconsin, Terri graduated from Seymour High School and the University of Wisconsin-Oshkosh. She was a reporter and editor at the *Oshkosh Northwestern* daily newspaper for five years before beginning her freelance writing career. In her spare time, Terri plays soccer and reads. She enjoys cross-country skiing and attending plays with her husband, Denis, and swimming, biking, and playing with their three children—Kyle, Rachel, and Emily.